The Pennsylvania-German Decorated Chest

The Pennsylvania-German Decorated Chest has been selected by The Pennsylvania German Society, Breinigsville, Pennsylvania, as volume 12 in their series of publications. Publication has been assisted by a grant from The Dietrich Brothers Americana Corporation.

MONROE H. FABIAN

The Pennsylvania-German Decorated Chest

FOREWORD BY
Pastor Frederick S. Weiser

A MAIN STREET PRESS BOOK

UNIVERSE BOOKS   NEW YORK

Library of Congress Catalog Card Number 77-91892

ISBN 0-87663-310-6

Published by Universe Books
381 Park Avenue South
New York City 10016

Produced by The Main Street Press
42 Main Street
Clinton, New Jersey 08809

Designed by Helen Tracy

Contents

FOREWORD by Pastor Frederick S. Weiser   13

THE PENNSYLVANIA-GERMAN
DECORATED CHEST

     The European Background   15

     The Chest in Pennsylvania   18

     Cabinetmaking and Woods   36

     Construction   38

     Hardware   43

     Surface Decoration   50

     Paint   52

     Decoration and Decorators   58

     Outside Pennsylvania   67

NOTES TO THE TEXT   72

ILLUSTRATIONS   81

NOTES TO ILLUSTRATIONS   217

SELECTED BIBLIOGRAPHY   222

INDEX   226

List of Illustrations

following page 80

1. Late Renaissance arcaded chest from the southern Tirol.

2. Carved oak chest from Schleswig-Holstein, 1751.

3. *Frontalstollentruhe* of carved oak from Borstel, 1694.

4. Small painted *Seitstollentruhe* from Switzerland, 1732.

5. *Kastentruhe* of painted softwood from near Kassel, 1758.

6. *Kastentruhe* of painted softwood from Württemberg, 1781.

7. Swiss *Kastentruhe* of painted softwood, 1782.

8. *Kastentruhe* of painted softwood from Alsace, 1849.

9. Engraving of a "Cloths Chest" in Thomas Chippendale's 1762 pattern book.

10. English chest over drawers, 18th century.

11. Chest over drawer from Bermuda, 18th century.

12. Berks County chest over drawers, c. 1800.

13. English chest over drawers with stepped construction, 18th century.

14. Pennsylvania chest over drawers with stepped construction, late 18th century.

15. Chest dated 1715 and a cradle, from near Freiburg, Switzerland.

16. Hinge from a chest dated 1764.

17. Late 18th-century chest hinge.

18. Hinge from a chest dated 1775.

19. Hinge from a chest dated 1773.

20. Chest hinge, c. 1780.

21. Hinge from a chest dated 1792.

22. Chest hinge, c. 1810.

23. Chest hinge, c. 1820.

24. Back of a chest dated 1764, showing portions of hinges.

25. Detail of the hinge on a chest dated 1785.

26. Carrying handle on a chest dated 1791.

27. Carrying handle on a chest dated 1775.

28. Crab lock on a chest dated 1764.

29. Box lock on a chest from the 1780's.

30. Working side of a drawer lock.

31. Keyhole plate on a chest dated 1764.

32. Key to a chest dated 1764.

33 and 34. Details of a pair of hinges signed "HS" and dated 1792.

35. Lock stamped "IOSEPH STVMB" on a chest dated 1757.

36. Lock stamped "W. CLEWELL" on an early 19th-century chest.

37. Plate from the Samuel Rowland Fisher hardware catalogue.

38. Plate from the Fisher catalogue.

39. Components of a brass drawer pull.

40. Pressed-brass drawer pull.

41. Maryland chest dated 1791.

42. Chest over drawers found in Ohio.

43. Chest found in Ohio.

44. Virginia chest attributed to Johannes Spitler.

45. Chest found in Virginia.

46. Scratched inscription on the chest from Virginia.

47. North Carolina chest dated 1793.

48. Chest on frame fround in North Carolina.

49. Chest made in Ohio or Indiana.

50. Schwenkfelder immigrant's chest, 1729.

51. Schwenkfelder immigrant's chest, not dated.

52. Inlaid Pennsylvania chest over drawers, 1757.

53. Chest, Lancaster County, 1764.

54. Chest, Lancaster County, 1765.

55. Detail of the 1765 chest.

56. Pennsylvania chest over drawers, 1765.

57. Lancaster County walnut chest with sulfur inlay, 1765.

58. Lancaster wardrobe, walnut with sulfur inlay, 1779.

59. Pennsylvania chest, 1768.

60. Berks County chest over drawers, 1769.

61. Chest over drawers, possibly Lehigh County, 1769.

62. Lehigh County chest, 1769.

63. Pennsylvania chest, 1770.

64. Front of a chest dated 1771(?).

65. End of the 1771(?) chest.

66. Chest, probably from Berks County.

67. Enameled *Humpen*, Franconia, 1675.

68. Pennsylvania chest over drawers, 1773.

69. Chest over drawers, probably from Berks County, 1786.

70. Chest over drawers, probably from Berks County, 1791.

71. Berks County chest with designs painted on bare wood.

72. Chest over drawers, probably from Berks County.

73. Berks County chest over drawers, 1803.

74. Centre County chest, 1806(?).

75. Pennsylvania chest, undated.

76. Walnut chest over drawers with pewter and wood inlay, 1773.

77. Pennsylvania arcaded chest, 1774.

78. Arcaded chest that may have been made for a couple, 1776.

79. Arcaded chest, 1774.

80. Flat board chest by the same maker, 1775.

81. Detail of Peter Rohn's signature on a chest dated 1784.

82. Chest over drawers, 1796, also possibly by Peter Rohn.

83. Chest decorated with cityscapes, 1775.

84. Chest with applied spindle decoration.

85. Berks County chest decorated with unicorns, 1778.

86. Arcaded chest decorated with flowers and pelicans.

87. Chest decorated with lions, initialed "AA".

88. Berks County chest decorated with unicorns, 1784.

89. Fully decorated Berks County chest, undated.

90. Detail of the end of the Berks County chest.

91. Chest over drawers with unicorn decoration, 1803.

92. Swiss nutwood chest with inlay, 17th century.

93. Painted box from the Alpachtal, c. 1750.

94. Mangel, Baden, 1737.

95. British coat of arms on a Philadelphia broadside, 1778.

96. Pennsylvania coat of arms on a document, 1782.

97. German glazed ceramic bowl, after 1757.

98. Plate from a Berks County six-plate stove, c. 1760.

99. *Exselenz Georg General Waschingthon*, watercolor, c. 1780.

100. Birth and baptismal certificate decorated with horses and riders, c. 1790.

101. Ceramic plate decorated with a horse and rider, attributed to Johannes Neesz, c. 1800–1825.

102. Pennsylvania chest decorated with horses and riders.

103. Lehigh County chest over drawers, 1777.

104. Walnut inlaid chest over drawers, 1777.

105. Christian Selzer chest, signed and dated 1777.

106. Detail of the signature and date.

107. John Selzer chest, signed and dated 1804.

108. John or Peter Rank chest, signed and dated 1800.

109. Chest decorated by one of the Rank family.

110. Chest over drawers by Michael Stoot, signed and dated 1788.

111. Stamp decorated chest, 1787.

112. Detail of one of the horsemen with swords on Johannes Trump's chest.

113. Chest over drawers from upper Berks County, 1779.

114. Upper Berks County chest, 1798.

115. Chest over drawers partially decorated with stencils, 1781.

116. Lancaster County chest of sycamore with sulfur and wood inlay, 1781.

117. Berks County walnut chest with contrasting inlay, 1783.

118. Berks County wardrobe of walnut with contrasting inlay, 1781.

119. Chest signed by the artist "HS", 1787.

120. Arcaded chest with double set of initials, 1787.

121. Chest probably from Lebanon County, 1784.

122. Arcaded chest over drawers, 1785.

123. Chest over drawers from Berks County, 1785.

124. Chest decorated with painted twisted columns, 1786.

125. Embossed cover of a German song book sold in Philadelphia, 1774.

126. Chest over drawers from near the Berks-Lehigh County line, 1788.

127. Lancaster County chest over drawers, 1786.

128. Chest over drawers by a Lancaster County decorator, 1788.

129. Another chest by the same unidentified decorator, 1805.

130. Detail of the lettering on the 1805 chest.

131. Chest over drawers from Bern Township, Berks County, 1788.

132. A later chest over drawers from the same workshop, dated 1796.

133. Detail from another chest from the same shop, undated.

134. Drawing of a *Hochzeitszug* from a late medieval manuscript.

135. Lancaster County chest, initialed by the decorator "J.F.", 1788.

136. Chest, 1788, attributed to the Lancaster County decorator, John Flory.

137. Chest over drawers of painted walnut attributed to Flory, 1791.

138. Painted softwood chest attributed to Flory, 1794.

139. Lancaster County chest over drawers, 1810.

140. Arcaded chest over drawers with unicorn decoration, 1788.

141. Lancaster or Montgomery County chest with tulip decoration, 1789.

142. Chest with decoration based upon work by the "Flat Tulip Artist."

143. Pen and ink and watercolor drawing attributed to Henrich Otto.

144. Detail of an end of the chest shown in Fig. 142.

145. Chest with freely brushed decoration.

146. Berks County chest, 1790.

147. Fragment of a chest over drawers with mermaid decoration, 1790.

148. Stone stove support, Württemberg, 1787.

149. Pennsylvania baptismal certificate with mermaid decoration, after 1811.

150. Chest over drawers from Lehigh or Bucks County.

151. Lehigh-Bucks chest over drawers by the same decorator.

152. Walnut chest with sulfur inlay, 1792.

153. Berks County chest for a member of the Himmelberger family.

154. Himmelberger chest dated 1793.

155. Painted wardrobe by the artist of the Himmelberger chests.

156. Chest over drawers decorated with cats.

157. Arcaded chest probably made in Berks County.

158. Chest over drawers of inlaid walnut, 1795.

159. Arcaded chest over drawers, 1795.

160. Unicorn decorated chest over drawers, 1797.

161. Chest over drawers with eagle decoration.

162. Reverse of the 1798 ten dollar gold piece.

163. Nineteenth-century chest with eagle decoration.

164. Chest, dated 1798 and numbered "Num 8."

165. Nineteenth-century chest with large heart decoration.

166. Centre County chest with bird and flower decoration.

167. Chest with painting of Adam and Eve.

168. Block decorated chest, 1804.

169. Chest over drawers from the Lykens Valley area.

170. Severely decorated chest probably from upper Bucks County.

171. Nineteenth-century Susquehanna Valley chest.

172. Chest over drawers from the Mahantango Valley, 1828.

173. Name panel on a Mahantango Valley chest.

174. Chest over drawers from the Manhantango Valley, 1812.

175. Mahantango Valley chest, 1814.

176. Nineteenth-century chest decorated with rosettes.

177. Chest with circle and floret decoration, 1816.

178. Chest over drawers with flower and house decoration.

179. Detail of a design of a bird eating cherries.

180. Chest over drawers with heart decoration, 1819.

181. Monroe County chest over drawers with a signed lock.

182. Chest over drawers from Montgomery County, 1823.

183. Montgomery County chest over drawers, 1829.

184. Later nineteenth-century chest over drawers.

185. Grained and smoke-decorated chest over drawers.

186. Mahantango Valley chest.

187. Birth and baptismal certificate printed in Lebanon, 1818.

188. Late Mahantango Valley chest over drawers, 1834.

189. One of a group of chests found in Centre County.

190. Grained chest, 1847.

191. Chest attributed to Joel Palmer.

192. End of a chest decorated by Joel Palmer.

193. Small chest attributed to Joel Palmer.

194. Chest signed by Christian Blauch, 1854.

195. Late style chest with owner's name, 1877.

196. Late Lancaster County chest over drawers, 1887.

197. Page from the Amish cabinetmaker Henry Lapp's design book.

198. Varnish grained chest over drawers, 1892.

199. Schwenkfelder immigrant's chest dated 1732.

200. Walnut chest over drawers with light wood inlay, 1741.

201. Arcaded chest found in Lancaster County, 1764.

202. Chest of painted softwood, 1769.

203. Chest with lengthy dialect inscription, 1773.

204. Lehigh County chest, 1776.

205. Chest over drawers probably made in Lehigh County, 1775.

206. Lehigh County chest, 1776.

207. Chest with stamped decoration, 1779.

208. Walnut chest over drawers with sulfur inlay, 1783.

209. Detail of a 1784 Berks County chest.

210. Chest signed by Christian Selzer and dated 1784.

211. Detail of a 1796 chest by Christian Selzer.

212. Chest over drawers signed by Johan Rank and dated 1790.

213. Lancaster County chest, 1782.

214. Chest probably painted in Lebanon County, 1784.

215. Chest with stepped construction, 1785.

216. Chest over drawers, 1786.

217. Detail of a chest painted in Lancaster County, 1788.

218. Printed and hand-drawn birth and baptismal certificate by Henrich Otto, 1784.

219. Chest with a six-panel painted front.

220. Stepped chest with dentil moulding above the drawers.

221. Chest over drawers with designs outlined in white, 1788.

222. Detail of the inscription on a Lancaster County chest.

223. Lancaster County chest, 1795.

224. Arcaded chest from Berks County, 1792.

225. Chest attributed to John Flory, 1791.

226. *Mrs. Washington*, engraving by John Norman, 1782.

227. Chest over drawers from Lehigh County, 1792.

228. Berks County chest over drawers, 1794.

229. Northampton County chest over drawers, 1795.

230. Berks County chest, 1795.

231. Chest with elaborate bird decoration, 1795.

232. Chest, probably from Berks County.

233. Bern Township, Berks County chest, 1799.

234. Detail of a round panel with star decoration.

235. Small-size boldly-decorated chest.

236. Chest over drawers from the Lizard Creek Valley, 1804.

237. Chest over drawers from near the Lehigh-Bucks County line, 1805.

238. Center panel of a chest over drawers, probably from Dauphin County, 1805.

239. Chest over drawers with sgraffito decoration.

240. Adam and Eve on an early nineteenth-century chest.

241. Lancaster County chest, 1818.

242. Chest with textured and geometric decoration.

243. Centre County chest with decoration based upon Fraktur.

244. Drawing of lions and flowers attributed to the "Flat Tulip Artist," c. 1800.

245. Chest over drawers with floral decoration, 1823.

246. Centre County chest with Allentown house blessing mounted inside lid.

247. Montgomery County chest with exceptional lettering, 1826.

248. Chest with sgraffito and brushed decoration.

249. Mid-nineteenth-century chest with framed construction.

250. Detail of sunflowers on a miniature chest by Joel Palmer.

Acknowledgments

My earliest memory of a Pennsylvania-German decorated chest is of seeing one at the auction Martha Hill Hommel held from her log-house antique shop in Pleasant Valley about 1949. The germ of this book is probably in that chest—a Berks County type if the vision is not too dim—being carried into the sun through the door of the shop. Later, at the University of Pennsylvania there was a thirty-five page paper about chests, written with some charming coaching by the late Frances Lichten. As we talked she drew wobbly little drawings for me with her left hand because her right was encased in a plaster cast. My notes and photos piled up and finally in 1971 Pastor Fred Weiser encouraged me to devote time to a serious study. He was but the first of many who have assisted me along the way to this finished work.

During my research in Germany, Eberhard Ander, Bernward Kalusche and Wilhelm Rokahr were kind enough to show me small museums they knew would be of interest. Many professional colleagues in the United States have been most generous with their support and assistance. At the Smithsonian Institution I must thank Rita Adrosko, Richard Ahlborn, Anne Golovin and Rodris Roth; at the Abby Aldrich Rockefeller Folk Art Center, Don Walters; at the Landis Valley Farm Museum, Carroll Hopf and Vernon S. Gunnion; at the Philadelphia Museum of Art, Beatrice Garvan; at the Henry Francis du Pont Winterthur Museum, Nancy Goyne Evans, Charles Hummel and Karol Schmiegel; and while Director of the Historical Society of York County, Harry Rinker. Among antiques dealers, Mildred and Ed Bohne, Harry Hartmann and David Pottinger have been especially helpful, as were Tillie and Mark Kohn, who have known me from the beginning of this project years ago and have always encouraged me in my work. The work of all the photographers represented in the book is genuinely appreciated and particularly that of Budd Gray, Max Hirshfeld and Eugene Mantie, friends who learned the finer points of furniture moving while working with me. Robert S. Gamble deserves credit for teaching me the value of the automobile as a research tool. Gregory Coster, Ralph Esmerian and Pastor Larry Neff always offered encouragement and hospitality. Don Yoder has been a valued friend and my mentor in all things *Pennsylvaanisch Deitsch* since my student days at the University of Pennsylvania. A special *vielen Danke* is reserved for Doris Rauch, without whom my German correspondence would have been sadly unintelligible.

Very special thanks are also in order for The Dietrich Brothers Americana Corporation, which provided grants that made possible both research in Europe and the production of color plates.

Washington, D.C.
October, 1977

MONROE H. FABIAN

Foreword

Much of the history that has bored generations of students has involved the small number of people whose names became important, who came from ruling or noble families, or whose descendants trace lineage back hundreds of years. But another sort of "history" has involved the peasant, the burgher, the "common man," who were often as not cannon fodder, certainly men of hard physical labor, and surely as anonymous as their forgotten graves. This is a book about something of the history of those anonymous persons.

In the years after the Thirty Years' War, a devastating, but surprisingly rejuvenating conflict in the heart of the Continent, the classes of people who fed that world began to strive upward. They adopted, in their own way, the sumptuousness of the upper classes. Their copies of upper-class wares, from furnishings to portraits to attire, are frequently grouped together under the name of *folk art*. These were the years when the masses began to see themselves as individuals, existing both in and apart from the groups of which they were members: the family, the village or *Dorf*, the Church, a region. In this period of history we find for the first time objects inscribed with their owners' names and owned by members of what developed as a middle class in the Western World. For now people had the resources to have things of their own.

One of the most engaging of such objects is the chest, about which this book is concerned. An ancient style of furniture, at once for sitting and for storage, the chest became the repository of an individual's goods: his (or her) clothes, linens, treasures. When in the eighteenth-century the Germans came in droves to America—to Pennsylvania—they brought the chest and the nascent individualism it represented with them. The majority of these pieces were either finished or simply painted, but the minority of inlaid or paint-decorated chests are the classic pieces of Pennsylvania-German decorative art to this day.

The chest often bore its owner's name and a date. Not infrequently the owner's *Taufschein* (baptismal certificate) and the fraktur drawings he had earned by learning his ABC's were stored in its till or pasted on the inside of the lid. A string hung on the same lid to hold its owner's stockings. Frequently acquired in its owner's adolescence, the chest then was something of a "dower" chest, as it was often called, filled with goods in anticipation of marriage. And after marriage it was still a personal piece of furniture used for clothing and blankets, a use which gave it its other common names. Its owners, however, never knew it as anything but a *Kischt*, their own chest, some of them proudly proclaiming, *"Diese Kist gehöret mier"*—This chest belongs to me.

But the lifetime of these documents in wood saw many another service. How many diapers were changed on their lids? How many little (or even big) feet scampered over them on their way to a high bed? How many hogs were butchered on them after they had been relegated from bedroom to summer kitchen? A terrible trick, one might say, to play on so noble an object, but perfectly logical to a folk who had things, no matter how pretty, to *use*, and not to look at. How many chests have been attacked by rodents because they contained grain and not the linens so carefully and exhaustingly made for the wedding bed?

This study by a scholarly Pennsylvania German, whose ancestors arrived at Philadelphia in 1732, fills a gap that has long been preempted by gossip and assumptions. Carefully picking his way through limited resources, often compounded by vague attributions of provenance, Monroe H. Fabian has produced an essay which answers questions with precise data. The Pennsylvania German Society, which has been studying and publishing material about America's largest colonial minority since its founding in 1891, is happy to commend this work to its members and friends of Pennsylvania-German culture everywhere.

Hanover
In der Greizwoch, 1977

PASTOR FREDERICK S. WEISER
Editor
The Pennsylvania German Society

The European Background

One of the most distinctive and distinguished manifestations of Pennsylvania-German arts and crafts is the painted furniture produced by the cabinetmakers of southeastern Pennsylvania in the eighteenth and nineteenth centuries. Of the many household items adorned with painted decoration the *Kischt* or storage chest and the *Shonk*[1] or wardrobe are the most noteworthy. The wardrobe was a communal piece of furniture used by the entire household. It is not so frequently found as the *Kischt*, a more private item of furniture. Being much larger, the wardrobe was also more expensive and naturally took up more space in the house. It was therefore not nearly so convenient as the chest. The word *Kischt* is a derivation of a word that is as ancient as the furniture form itself. It comes from the Greek κιστη by way of the Latin *Cista* and the old-fashioned German word *Kiste*. The rectangular storage container with a lift-top lid has been called by various names throughout the German-speaking areas of Europe. *Lade* was heard in northern German dialects and *Kasten, Drog,* or *Trog* in the south. In modern standard German the word *Truhe* is that most commonly used. In Pennsylvania, however, it is the word *Kiste*, so common in the Palatinate homeland of many who came to America, and its dialect variant *Kischt*, that became the terms most often used for the storage chest found in virtually every home.

The genealogy of the Pennsylvania-German decorated chest begins with the German and Swiss chests of the late Middle Ages and the Renaissance (Fig. 1). Although these are often of a monumental size, befitting their use in a castle or in the large town house of an affluent merchant, the construction is basically the same as that of their humbler descendants. They are essentially storage boxes—sometimes over drawers—fitted with lift-top lids. The lids are usually attached with long and often elaborately-worked iron hinges. The exterior surfaces of the chests can be samplers of decorative techniques. These large and elaborate chests in the houses of the wealthy were emulated by the lower classes, but out of necessity scaled down in both size and ornamentation.

The chests belonging to the rich were covered with all manner of carving or intarsia or inlay. When they could be managed by the craftsmen or afforded by the customers, these techniques continued to be used by the small-town cabinetmakers who worked in hardwoods (Fig. 2). This, of course, was not the case all over Germany. Although the members of the formal cabinetmakers' guilds generally worked in hardwood, the smaller independent cabinet shop owners frequently worked in whatever wood was easiest to obtain.[2] In northwestern Germany, as far south as where the Rhine flows through the Palatinate, this wood was most often a hardwood, quite frequently oak. In south, central, and eastern Germany, as indeed over most of Europe from the middle Rhine to western Russia and from Scandinavia to the Alps, the wood most often used was a softwood.[3]

Regardless of the wood from which they were made, chests were the most important pieces of storage furniture in the German peasant houses through the seventeenth and eighteenth centuries, and they were found in many areas of the home. Some were used for storing foodstuffs such as smoked meats and dried fruits and were naturally found in larders and kitchens.[4] Some stood in the *Stube* or sitting room, filled with flax to be spun and yarn to be knitted.[5] The finely decorated chests, however, were chests for linens and clothes and stood usually in the *Kammer* or principal bed chamber.[6] Acquired by both young men and women—often long before the time of their marriage—at least this one piece of furniture, a clothes chest, sometimes came into newly wedded couples' homes in company with a wardrobe decorated to match. Both items of furniture were probably made on commission and were most likely decorated by the cabinetmaker who made them.[7]

Within the two German woodworking areas, several forms of the chest were in use during the seventeenth and eighteenth centuries. One of these was the *Stollentruhe*, of doweled tongue-and-groove construction and generally of hardwood. A *Stollentruhe* can be either a

Frontal-Stollentruhe (Fig. 3), on which the corner posts extend to the floor to form the "feet," or it can be a *Seit-Stollentruhe* (Fig.4). On the chests of this second form the front, back, and bottom are set into the plank ends which continue down to become the supports. The *Stollentruhe* was a form much more common in the north of Germany than in the south. Its very appearance tells us that it is an ancient form. In Germany the *Stollentruhe* was, indeed, already considered a very old-fashioned type of chest in the eighteenth century, and it belonged to the work realm of the carpenter. Being of hardwood, the *Stollentruhe* was more frequently carved than painted, although some carving was emphasized with touches of paint.[8]

The other important form of chest made in the seventeenth and eighteenth centuries is the *Kastentruhe* (Figs. 5, 6 and 7). It is in the form of a box set either directly on the floor without supports, or upon runners, turned feet, or a *Sockel*, usually one-half to two-fifths of the height of the chest. The more ancient form of this support is made of four boards doweled or otherwise joined at the corners. The box of the chest rests in it, but is not necessarily permanently joined to it. The corners of the chest proper may be joined by doweling or by dovetailing. The second is the more frequently used method. The *Kastentruhe*, constructed of planed boards joined together, was considered the work of the cabinetmaker. Since they were mostly constructed of softwoods, it is the *Kastentruhe* form that is most often the type of chest found with painted decorations. It is this form, with or without the various supports, which is overwhelmingly prevalent in Pennsylvania.[9] In fact, only in the nineteenth century, after decades of influence from British joinery, did the construction of any Pennsylvania decorated chests even approximate the construction details of the classic *Stollentruhe*.

The painted decoration of Germanic furniture began in Upper Bavaria in the early seventeenth century with a rather cautious use of stenciled patterns in black on natural wood. Only in the late eighteenth and early nineteenth centuries did the freehand polychrome painting on a white or colored ground blossom to its fullest expression.[10] Dated examples of chests from various regions of the German lands show that painted furniture of a fully developed type was definitely in use in the early eighteenth century—the time of the most frequent migration to America. It is evident, though, that the finest and most intricately decorated specimens of German painted furniture date from the late eighteenth and the early nineteenth centuries. This makes the high point of the art form in Europe contemporaneous with the development and decline of painted furniture in Pennsylvania. Although German furniture decoration in America seems to have developed fully side by side with the same techniques in Europe, a decline came sooner in the rural areas of the New World than of the Old. By the beginning of the third decade of the nineteenth century, Pennsylvania-German furniture decoration in the classic mode was all but ended. In Europe, however, the traditional forms continued to be made until the advent of the present century. Being less restricted from mobility across the strata of society than his European counterpart, the Pennsylvania-German farmer was freer to espouse the tastes and trappings of the urban middle class at an earlier date. Consequently, the painted "peasant" furniture in Pennsylvania farmhouses was replaced as soon as possible with veneered furniture in a countrified "American Empire" style. The form of the traditional German *Kischt*, however, did manage to survive in the Pennsylvania-German household into the twentieth century. By this time, though, the chests were devoid of all but the most anemic of embellishments.

The Chest in Pennsylvania

Chests of the German fashion first appeared in great number in Pennsylvania in the freight of the immigrants. The immigration began in 1683 with the arrival of Francis Daniel Pastorius and the handful of families who founded Germantown, a short distance north of Philadelphia. More Germans came during the next three decades, and by 1717 the tide of immigration had swelled to such proportions that the Provincial Council of Pennsylvania felt constrained to compose legislation regulating the admission and naturalization of Europeans who were not British subjects.[11] No other legal action appears to have been taken for another decade, and then on September 14, 1727, the Council, dismayed at the arrival of a ship bearing 400 refugees from the German lands, ordered that lists be made of all arriving immigrants.[12] On the basis of the lists which survive in the Pennsylvania State Archives, an estimated 60,000 Germans entered Pennsylvania through the port of Philadelphia between 1727 and 1775.[13]

Most likely, a majority of the immigrants brought their belongings in wooden chests. Some of these would have been purchased especially for the journey. Such was the case with Johann Phillip Hörner of Vockenroth who, in preparing for his trip to America, purchased a new chest for 3 florins. This was cheaper than the cost of the goatskin for pants which was priced at 5 florins or the one-quarter pail of brandy which was priced at 4 florins, 30 kreuzer.[14] Hörner made the transatlantic crossing safely and arrived at Philadelphia on October 31, 1786, aboard the brig *Dispatch* with his wife and three children.[15]

Early immigrants rarely left a written record of their journeys; but because they were so often victimized by the ship captains and their crews, there is documentation, pathetic as it is, of the shipping of belongings to Pennsylvania. How easy it is now—when a trip by air from Philadelphia to Frankfurt takes only seven hours—to look back and consider the eighteenth-century travelers either naïve or unintelligent. They were indeed naïve, for most of them had probably never been more than a few miles from their homes prior to the beginning of the long and arduous journey to the New World. Being untutored in the ways of the traveler and those who preyed on them, the immigrants trusted in the German agents who "acted in their behalf." Many of the agents were unscrupulous men who bled what money they could from the travelers all along the Rhine and in the Dutch ports from which they would eventually sail. Many were the families who had to sell themselves into indentured servitude when they reached Pennsylvania penniless.

Considerable numbers of the German travelers who were lucky enough to reach Philadelphia alive must have lamented that they had ever left home. Many of those who were strong enough to withstand the rigors of the Atlantic crossing under crowded conditions in filthy ships complained bitterly of being victimized all along the way. Their complaints, voiced often through concerned friends in Pennsylvania, are our principal source of information about the hazards of shipping one's belongings and the importation of the German chest.

Being neophyte travelers—often with no real understanding of the length of their pending journey—many were talked into having their chests sent on separate vessels. They paid for the naïveté. In 1749 this short, but informative, item appeared in the Germantown newspaper:

> The ships on which so many persons had put their chests [*ihre Kisten*], and which were so long in coming over, arrived on the 9th and 11th of the present month in Philadelphia. We hear that many of the chests were broken open. It is customary that when a ship captain receives goods and wares for delivery, he must turn them over to the owner as he receives them when the freight is paid, and what is lacking must be made good by him. But the Germans pay and must pay when their chests are robbed or when famished with hunger, even though their contracts are expressly to the contrary.[16]

So rapacious was the avarice of the ship captains and crews and so pitiful the suffering of the German immigrants that Christopher Sauer, a spokesman for the Pennsylvania-German community, wrote to Governor Robert Morris to complain.[17] Sauer, himself an immigrant, championed the cause of his countrymen in two letters which are our most important documentation concerning the importation of German chests and their use en route to America.[18] In his first letter, dated March 15, 1755, he dwells upon the destitution of the immigrants because of the thievery of ship captains and crews, and he mentions chests only once.

> The poor people on board are prisoners. They durst not go ashore, or have their chests delivered, except they allow in a bond or pay what they owe not. . . .[19]

In a second lengthy letter, dated at Germantown, May 12, 1755, Sauer underscores and condemns the prevalent practice of pillaging immigrants' baggage. This second letter is the most important documentation we have concerning the bringing of German chests to America. Not only does it give an indication of the hundreds—perhaps thousands—of pieces of furniture brought here in the eighteenth century, but it also lists for us the kinds of things stored in them during the voyages. It is rather surprising to read that many of the chests—

which we usually consider clothes chests—contained foodstuffs. Providing quantities of edibles for a long trip makes sense, of course, and it is suspected that food and clothes were packed in separate containers.

Honored and Beloved Sir:

Although I do believe with sincerity, that you have at this time serious and troublesome business enough,[20] nevertheless, my confidence in your wisdom makes me to write the following defective lines, whereby I desire not so much as a farthing of profit for myself.

When I heard last that the Assembly adjourned, I was desirous to know what was done concerning the Dutch bill and was told that your Honor have consented to all points, except that the German passengers need not have their chests along with them; and because you was busy with more needful business, it was not ended. I was sorry for it, and thought, either your Honor has not good counsellers or you can't think of the consequences, otherwise you could not insist on this point. Therefore I hope you will not take it amiss to be informed of the case, and of some of the consequences, viz.:—The crown of England found it profitable to peopling the American colonies; and for the encouragement thereof, the coming and transportation of German Protestants was indulged, and orders were given to the officers at the customhouses in the parts of England, not to be sharp with the vessels of German passengers—knowing that the populating of the British colonies will, in time become, profit more than the trifles of duty at the customhouses would import in the present time. This the merchants and importers experience.

They filled the vessels with passengers and as much of the merchant's goods as they thought fit, and left the passengers' chests &c behind, and sometimes they loaded vessels wholly with Palatines' chests. But the poor people depended upon their chests, wherein was some provision, such as they were used to, as dried-apples, pears, plums, mustard, medicines, vinegar, brandy, gammons, butter, clothing, shirts and other necessary linens, money and whatever they brought with them; and when their chests were left behind, or were shipped in some other vessel they had lack of nourishment. When not sufficient provision was shipped for the passengers, and they had nothing themselves, they famished and died. When they arrived alive, they had no money to buy bread, nor anything to sell. If they would spare clothes, they had no clothes or shirt to strip themselves, nor were they able to cleanse themselves of lice and nastiness. If they were taken into houses, trusting on their effects and money, when it comes, it was left behind, or robbed and plundered by the sailors behind or in the vessels. If such a vessel arrived before them, it was searched by the merchants' boys,

&c., and their best effects all taken out, and no remedy for it, and this last mentioned practice, that people's chests are opened and their best effects taken out, is not only a practice this twenty five, twenty, ten or five years, or sometime only; but it is the common custom and daily complaints to the week last past; when a pious man, living with me, had his chest broken open and three fine shirts and a flute taken out. The lock was broken to pieces and the lid of the chest split with iron and chisels. Such, my dear Sir, is the case, and if your honor will countenance the mentioned practices, the consequences will be, that the vessels with passengers will be filled with merchant's goods, wine, &c., as much as possible, and at the King's custom they will call it passengers' drink, and necessaries for the people, then household goods, &c., which will be called free of duty. And if they please to load the vessels only with chests of passengers and what lies under them, that will be called also free of duty at the customhouses; and as there are no owners of the chests with them, and no bill of loading is ever given, nor will be given, the chests will be freely opened and plundered by the sailors and others, and what is left will be searched in the stores by the merchants' boys and their friends and acquaintances. Thus, by the consequence, the King will be cheated, and the smugglers and store boys will be glad of your upholding and encouraging this, their profitable business; but the poor sufferers will sigh or carry a revenge in their bosoms, according as they are godly or ungodly, that such thievery and robbery is maintained.

If such a merchant should lose thirty, forty, fifty or ten thousand pounds, he may have some yet to spend and to spare, and has friends, but if a poor man's chest is left behind or plundered either at sea or in the stores he has lost all he has. If a rich man's store, or house, or chest is broken open and robbed or plundered there is abundance of noise about it; but if 1,000 poor men's property is taken from them, in the manner mentioned, there is not a word to be said.[21]

If I were ordered to print advertisements of people who lost their chests, by leaving them behind against their will, or whose chests were opened and plundered at sea, when they were sent after them in other vessels, or whose were opened and plundered in the stores of Philadelphia—should come and receive their value for it, (not four fold) but only single or half; your honor would be wondering of a swarm from more than two or three thousand people. But as such is not to be expected, it must be referred to the decision of the great, great, long, long day, where certainly an impartial judgement will be seen, and the last farthing must be paid, whereas in this present time, such poor sufferers has, and will have no better answer than is commonly given: "Can you prove who has opened and stolen out of your chest?" or "Have you a bill of loading?" this has been the practice by some of the merchants of Philadelphia, and if it must continue longer, the

Lord our God must compare that city to her sister Sodom, as he said: "Behold this was the iniquity of Sodom: pride, fullness of bread and abundance of idleness was in her. Neither did she strengthen the hand of the poor and needy (Ezekiel, 16:40) but rather weakened the hand of the poor and needy (18:2)."

As if he had not already said enough to plead the case of his countrymen, Sauer added a bold close to his letter.

> The Lord bless our good King and all his faithful ministers, and your Honor, and protect the city of Philadelphia and country from all incursions and attempts of enemies. But if you should insist against a remedy for the poor Germans' grievances—although no remedy is to be had for that which is past—and an attempt of enemies should ensue before the city of Philadelphia, you will certainly find the Germans faithful to the English nation;[22] as you might have seen how industrious they are to serve the King and government, for the protection of their substance, life and liberties. But, as there are many and many thousands who have suffered injustice of their merchants at Philadelphia, it would not be prudent to call on them all for assistance, as there are certainly many wicked among the Germans; which, if they should find themselves overpowered by the French, I would not be bound for their behaviour, that they would not make reprisals on them that picked their chests and forced them to pay what they owed not! and hindered yet the remedy for others. No! if they were all Englishmen who suffered so much, I would much less be bound for their good behaviour.

> Pray sir do not look upon this as a trifle; for there are many Germans, who have been wealthy people and many Germans, who have lost sixty, eighty, one, two, three, four hundred to a thousand pounds' worth, by leaving their chests behind, or were deprived and robbed in the stores, of their substance, and are obliged now to live poor, with grief. If you do scruple the truth of this assertion, let them be called in the newspaper, with hopes for remedies, and your Honor will believe me; but if the Dutch [German] nation should hear that no regard is for them, and no justice to be obtained, it will be utterly in vain to offer them free schools[23]—especially as they are to be regulated and inspected by one who is not respected in all this Province.

> I hope your Honor will pardon my scribbling; as it has no other aim than a needful redressing of the multitude of grievances of the poor people, and for the preserving of their lives and property, and that the Germans may be adhered to the friendship of the English nation, and for securing the honor of your Excellency, and not for a farthing for your humble servant.

Christopher Saur
Printer of Germantown[24]

This is hardly scribbling, but rather polite, unsubtle, militant prose from the pen of a peaceable printer, a member of the Church of the Brethren. Governor Morris may have silently smirked at Sauer's impudence when he read the letter in May of 1755—if indeed he ever read it.

Other letters and documents of the immigration period that mention chests are exceedingly rare. One other that has been discovered, however, is actually an inventory of the possessions brought in one of the chests. The immigrant, Lucina Keyser, came to Pennsylvania from Wertheim in the Frankenland of Baden, and evidently died shortly after her arrival. There is both an inventory of her possessions and a list of the prices paid for each item at the auction held after her death. Of the forty-seven items, only ten are not clothes or other fabrics. With the exception of a feather bed and two bolsters, all could have been stored in the average-size chest.

The inventory reads as follows:

May the Sixtanth 1757
Bresment of all the Goods Rights Chattells and Credis of the Deceased Lewisina Keiser in the Township of Upper Milford County of Northampton and Being as folwoeth Viz

	£	S	p
in Cash	2	0	0
To a Father Bed	0	16	0
To 2 Boulsters	0	3	0
To 3 Boulsters	0	4	0
To a Sheet for a Bed	0	4	0
To a Bed Cais	0	8	0
To i Boulster Cace	0	4	0
To Bed Cordence	0	1	0
To a Table Cloth	0	3	0
To a hand Towel	0	0	10
To a ? Blue Bede Coat	0	6	0
To a Strippet Bede Coat	0	6	0
To a Reddich Bede Coat	0	3	0
To a Black Bede Coat	0	7	0
To 2 Black aporns	0	2	0
To 2 Blue aporns	0	2	6
To a Black Jacket	0	1	0
To a Reddich womans Jacket	0	1	3
To a Bodis	0	2	6

To a Blue Bodis	0	0	6
To a pair Whit stockings one pair Red Dito	0	1	0
To a psalm Book	0	2	
To a Little Bible	0	4	0
To a Smothen Box and two ___ ?	0	1	0
	6	8	7
To a Silk hengerchif	0	2	0
To a Silk hengerchif	0	3	0
To a White hengerchif	0	1	6
To a pair of White Mittinds	0	0	8
To a pair of Clofes Blue To a pair Black Dito	0	0	9
To 2 Kaps for Women	0	0	6
To 3 Shmal Linin pisie of Nidel work	0	0	4
To a Box	0	0	2
To a Tine Bason	0	1	6
To a Copper Cetel	0	2	6
To a Tine Pint	0	0	2
To a Chist	0	2	0
To a Erthen Pot	0	0	2
To a Erthen Pot	0	0	3
	£17	4	i

After this appraisal, the "estate" of Lucina Keyser was sold at auction on July 2, 1757. Sold piece by piece, the items brought only 10 £ 10s. 9d. The "Chist" itself sold for 9s. 3d.[25]

Whatever their function on the voyage from Europe, many of the chests would have served their owners during the rest of their lives in America. This continued use of European-made furniture probably explains why so few chests of Pennsylvania manufacture—dateable before the 1760's—have been found.[26]

Only three chests have been recorded which have a tradition of having been brought to Pennsylvania by eighteenth-century immigrants. All three are said to have arrived with the Schwenkfelder immigration of 1734 and to have remained in family hands until they were given to the Schwenkfelder Museum, Pennsburg, Pennsylvania. They are all constructed of softwood—probably pine—and are painted. When color transparencies of the chests were sent to the *Museum für Deutsche Volkskunde* in West Berlin, two of the three were identified as having been made in Saxony (Figs. 50 and 199). The chest dated 1729 was thought to be of Saxon manufacture because of the characteristic green background and floral decoration. The chest dated 1732 was placed even more closely. This latter chest is believed to have come from the area of Herrnhut, the headquarters of the *Unitas Fratrum* or Moravian Church. There is every possibility that at least this one chest was actually made and decorated in the *Bruder-haustischlerei* in Herrnhut itself. This cabinet shop did not only routine construction carpentry, but also high-style furniture in the English taste and painted furniture to satisfy the taste of the villagers living nearby. Since the Schwenkfelders were under the protection of Count Nicholas von Zinzindorf, the leader of the Moravians, from 1725 until the time of their emigration to Pennsylvania in 1734, the stylistic evidence would seem to support the tradition concerning ownership. The third chest (Fig. 51), undated, could only be placed in time somewhere in the first half of the eighteenth century on the basis of decoration and construction. Because of its rather freely brushed decoration, a point of origin could not be stated with certainty. One suspects that it is also Saxon.[27]

From the time of the earliest arrival of the German immigrants until about the end of the eighteenth century, the chest with a lift-top lid remained the most important item of storage furniture in the rural homes of southeastern Pennsylvania. Only gradually was it replaced by the chest of drawers introduced to America by the English settlers.

The chest of drawers or the chest-on-chest was the preeminent piece of storage furniture for the urbane eighteenth-century Englishman in both the British Isles and in America. Although Thomas Chippendale included an illustration of at least one lift-top-lid chest in his 1762 pattern book (Fig. 9),[28] this form of furniture had been considered old-fashioned by mid-century in stylish urban circles. For centuries the chest had an honorable history in British homes. It was a quite important piece of storage furniture throughout the late Tudor and early Stuart periods—as it had been in the Middle Ages—even though the cupboard with doors had become popular by that time. In the late sixteenth century, however, innovations in furniture style signaled the decline of the popularity of the chest. At that time chests with drawers begin to be mentioned with regularity in English inventories. Known now as "mule chests," an appellation that may be of nineteenth-century origin, they were little more than the box-like ancient chest form with one or two drawers at the bottom. From these pieces of furniture evolved the true chest of drawers which first appeared about the middle of the sixteenth century. After the Restoration in 1660, they were in wide use in the more fashionable homes, and by the early eighteenth century they were the dominant form of storage furniture in the households of the affluent. At the turn of the century the double chest of drawers or chest-on-chest also appeared. There was a revival of the ancient chest form in that century, too, but the resultant pieces of furniture were frequently ornate, in sarcophagus form, and were intended more for interior decoration than for hard use.[29] Outside of the high-style centers of the British Isles and the Continent, however, it was otherwise, and country cabinetmakers, not so easily swayed by the swift changes of fashion in the cities, continued to make the "old-fashioned" chest. As recent scholarship has shown, the fact must not be overlooked that even some urban folk were country people at heart when it came to furnishing their homes. It is simply possible that some of the plainer and, therefore, cheaper eighteenth-century furniture from both England and America now called "country furniture" may actually have been made in urban workshops for clients of simpler tastes or modest means.[30]

From the first quarter of the seventeenth century until about the second of the nineteenth, a number of hinged-top chests were also made in another of England's American colonies, Bermuda. Constructed of cedar, the earliest is thought to date from about 1623. Most of these chests are set on a low frame, very unlike anything known to have been made in Pennsylvania by any of the German cabinetmakers. Others rest on turned feet (Fig. 11). The most distinguishing detail of the cedar chests from Bermuda is the very intricate dovetailing. The spiky patterns are a nice grace note on an otherwise unadorned surface of natural wood. Probably because most or all of the chests remained on the island or went to England, these chests appear to have had no influence on other American furniture craftsmen.[31] They are, however, now sometimes mistaken for pieces made on the mainland.

In Pennsylvania, relatively few chests have been found which bear dates prior to 1770. Of course, this does not mean that many may not have been made before that time. Chests which are not dated are frequently impossible to place chronologically. Styles changed so slightly during the course of the eighteenth century, especially in rural areas, that a chest which seems to have been made around 1750 might just as well have been constructed circa 1795.

It is possible, however, that the paucity of chests dated prior to 1770 is an indication that relatively few were indeed constructed in this country at an early date. It is not impossible that the first and even second generation of Pennsylvania Germans utilized furniture that the family had brought with them from Europe when they emigrated.

Until the chest of drawers became the major piece of storage furniture in German households, as it was in the English, each family member apparently had his or her own chest. That such chests were considered personal pieces of property can be readily sensed by observing the number which bear the names or initials of the original owners. On the basis of the life dates of those original owners who can be identified, it appears that the chests were acquired in the early or mid-teenage years or at the time of marriage. Thus, both young men and women received chests at about the time they would have become old enough to be responsible for their own belongings. The young men's chests probably held mainly clothes and whatever small treasures they had managed to accumulate. The girls' storage chests would have been filled with both clothes and other fabrics to be taken along to new homes after marriage.

Although there was no compelling legal reason for a parent in Pennsylvania to provide any sort of marriage gift for children about to be married, such gift giving was a custom widely practiced in the eighteenth and nineteenth centuries. Men were sometimes given one or two pieces of furniture as part of their inheritance prior to marriage; most often their gifts were in the form of money or farm animals and equipment. Furniture, fabrics, and other household goods such as pots and pans and cutlery were a major part of the marriage gift given to women. Since the chest was a primary piece of storage furniture in a Pennsylvania-German house, it was almost always included with the furnishings used by the bride in her new home. It was included with the marriage furniture because it was a personal piece of furniture, and not because it was considered to be a "dower chest."

Given the native conservatism of the German immigrants, it is not at all surprising to find that the custom of the *Aussteuer* or marriage gift was retained as tenaciously as were the dialects and religions of this transplanted people. From the Middle Ages until the time of the great immigration to America, the collection of the *Aussteuer* was a major activity for every young German girl preparing for marriage. The idea of a marriage gift, or "dowry" as it is so often called in common parlance, had evidently been taken over from the sumptuous practices of the nobility and had been given a more modest cast by the lower classes.[32] Among the merchant and farming classes the marriage gift assumed a modicum of magnificence proportionate to the wealth of each family. In some cases the accumulation of goods to be taken to the home of the newly wedded couple was substantial. In other cases the young couple had to make do with only a few necessities. In this respect, life was no different in America than it had been in Europe.

There are references to the idea of the *Aussteuer* or marriage portion in more than a few Pennsylvania-German documents—mostly wills and account books. In November of 1790, Phillip Himmelberger of Tulpehocken Township, Berks County, showed concern for the marriage portion of his offspring when he wrote:

> Item I order that my two Daughters, who are yet unmarried, shall have equal House-furniture in the manner with the one that is married.

Mindful of giving each child an equal settlement of goods, he was also concerned for his wife's property when he added:

> . . . I bequeth unto my dear widow . . . the wedding bed, her chest with all linen, which is in it, twenty pounds of flax, twenty pounds of tow, and the kitchen closet.[33]

It is not inconceivable—in fact, it is most likely—that at least the chest and the kitchen closet were part of the widow-to-be's marriage gift from her father.

Care was taken that gifts comprised of both money and goods to one child should equal gifts of money alone to another. John George Wolfesbarger, a concerned father living in Lebanon County, clearly spelled out his care for fair apportionment when he wrote his will in 1816:

. . . I have already given and advanced unto my Daughter Catharine in Furniture & c. the Sum of Two Hundred Dollars, and to my Daughter Eve the Sum of twenty five Dollars and I give her the said Eve, the further Sum of One Hundred and Seventy five Dollars. . . .[34]

The desire to apportion fairly was still prevalent in mid-century when, in 1842, Benjamin Schmoyer of Lower Macungie Township, Lehigh County, used the dialect form *aus steier* in writing in his account book concerning the inheritance of his children:

> 1842, den 1ten Merz had ich meinem Sohn Daniel seinen *aus steier* gegeben vor dieses mahl, und so soll ein Jedes haben wie das Andern in Gleigen Theil vom Elsten bis zum Juengsten. Das ist mein Willen und Testament— so viel von mier.
> [1842, the 1st of March, I have given my son Daniel his *aus steier* before this time, and so shall each have as the other in like portion from the oldest to the youngest. This is my Will and Testament—so much from me.][35]

Daniel, one of Schmoyer's nine children, received only one piece of furniture as part of his gift—a bed. In 1837, the oldest daughter, Mary Jane, received seventy dollars' worth of *Schreiner arbeit* or cabinet-work, and three other sons each received *ein Scketerri*. This last item is probably a "secretary" or desk with bookcase above.[36]

The most informative documentation concerning the Pennsylvania-German practice of a marriage portion in the eighteenth and nineteenth centuries is found in the Clemens family account book, a small volume used by three generations of a relatively well-to-do Mennonite family in Salford Township, Montgomery County.[37] The progenitor of the line in America was Gerhart Clemens (1680–1745) who emigrated in 1709.[38] It was his son Jacob (1707?–1782) who wrote the first entries in the book, followed by the grandson Gerhart II (1743–1820) and the great-grandson Henrich (1783–1869). Jacob Clemens's entries in the book include, among the everyday expenses and transactions of farm life, itemized lists of those things he purchased for the nine daughters married between 1749 and 1778. This accumulation of goods was indeed no mean feat and is an obvious indication of the wealth of the family.

It should be noted that each of Jacob Clemens's three sons was also provided with a gift before or at the time of his marriage. Each received an outlay of cash and a few farming or household items. In no case was the gift to a son composed of any substantial set of furniture, or of nearly as many items as were given to the daughters. As was usual, the fathers of all three generations took great pains to insure that each of the children received gifts—either in cash or goods—of equal value.

Jacob Clemens begins the first entry relative to a daughter's gifts with the notation:

> Anno 1749 d 17 Dag Augustÿ haben Wir unserer dochter Anna Clemensin hochzeit gehalten [.] Nun ferner zeige ich hir mit an wasz wir ihr mit gegeben haben zur hausz Steüer und anfang zur haus Haltung näbes seinen kleiteren. . . .
>
> [August 17, 1749, we had the wedding for our daughter Anna Clemens. I will now enumerate what we gave her as a dowry to begin housekeeping, besides her clothes. . . .][39]

He then proceeds to itemize bedding, wooden goods, pewter, copper, iron, and livestock. The first items mentioned under *höltzgen häusz roth* (woodenware) are *eine böttlade* (a bedstead) and *eine Peindt küst mit zweij schubladen mit schlosz und bänder* (a pine chest with two drawers with lock and hinges). Subsequently, Jacob wrote out the same kind of inventory for each of his nine daughters married between 1749 and 1778. The last inventory, written for his daughter Susanna, mentions no furniture at all, only fabrics, tinware, a cow, a bridle, and a saddle. Since there is no record of Susanna's marriage, the lack of furniture may reflect the fact that she was living at home.[40]

Of the nine girls, six received a chest; four, a table; three, a dough trough; seven, a bed; six, a dish cupboard; and one, a clothes wardrobe. Allowing for items missed when copying from loose notes into the bound book or for missing book pages, it is evident that the bed, the cupboard, and the chest were the types of furniture most often given. Of the last three girls married, only one received any piece of clothes storage furniture—a wardrobe. An examination of the inventories also shows that, strangely enough, no seating furniture of any kind, neither chairs nor benches, was part of any of the sets of dowry furniture.

A brief description and a listing of the prices paid for most of the chests is included in the Clemens inventories. A chest bought in 1749 is of pine with two drawers, but no cost is given. In 1751, no wood is listed, but the chest has two drawers and the cost is £1.10.0. In this same year the cupboard costs only £0.8.0., and even four sheep, at £1.8.0, are cheaper than the chest. In 1755 the chest is pine with two drawers and costs £1.5.0. The following year no wood is mentioned, but drawers are noted, almost certainly two or three, and the cost again is £1.5.0. In 1763 the chest is of walnut, drawers are mentioned, and the cost is £1.16.0. In 1773 no wood is mentioned, no drawers are mentioned, but the cost is £2. Even so the chest is cheaper than a copper kettle which is priced at £2.16.0. This last chest may have been priced higher than all the others mentioned because of some unde-scribed elaborate detail of construction. There is no mention of any painted or inlaid decoration. It is quite possible, however, that all the pine pieces were at least painted with a ground color to protect the wood.

The reader of the Clemens inventories must not overlook the im-portance of the listing of prices. The very mention of cost implies that the furniture was not made by members of the family, but was pur-chased from craftsmen living off the farm.

By the time of the marriage of the first daughter of Gerhart Clem-ens II in 1792, the only piece of clothes storage furniture mentioned in the inventories is a *Kleider Shank* or wardrobe. No chest is mentioned as having been purchased for any of the four girls of that generation, nor is there any mention of the chest of drawers.[41] The chest of drawers was clearly the favored piece of storage furniture by the time the first girl of the next generation of the family married. Balle, the first of Henrich Clemens's daughters to marry, received in 1826, as did her three sisters, not a *Kischt* or a *Kleider Schank*, but a chest of drawers. These pieces of furniture out of the English tradition are variously listed in the inventories as a *Draar*, a *Trar*, and a *Traar*. All three words are quite obviously formed from a German pronunciation of the English word "drawer." If a chest was used by the families set-ting up housekeeping in this generation, it was probably second-hand, or at least was not purchased as part of the furniture given with the marriage gift.

To point out that the chest was replaced in the Clemens family by the chest of drawers is not to imply that the older furniture form fell completely out of favor in the Pennsylvania-German community as a whole. In fact, as is indicated by many surviving nineteenth-century examples, the simpler form has been used almost to the present day. The author's great-aunt, now 103-years-old, has told how her parents bought her a chest when she was in her teens in upper Bucks County in the 1880's. Similarly, the women of the family born just after 1900 were given chests when they were teenagers. By the 1920's, however, the chests were not purchased from country cabinetmakers, but from a furniture store in Bethlehem. Devoid of any decoration, the chests are simple cedar chests and still remain in constant use.

One scholar, writing recently of the Old Order Mennonites of eastern Pennsylvania, has observed:

> In anticipation of her wedding the girl has been accumulating items for a number of years. Somewhere between the ages of fifteen and seventeen every girl receives a hope chest from her parents. These chests are never purchased new at a furniture store but are either homemade by a member of the family or acquired at an auction sale. The chief purpose of the hope chest is to serve as a repository for the many quilts given to the girl by her mother and sisters.[42]

The term "hope chest," in common use since the early decades of this century, is not a term that appears ever to have been used earlier by the Pennsylvania Germans either in German or in English. It is a term that is probably a product of late-Victorian sentimentality.

As a piece of furniture for the storage of clothes and personal possessions, the chest was associated with the sleeping and robing rooms of a house. The *Kammer*, or bedchamber, is indeed where it was most often kept in the Pennsylvania-German house—space permitting. One of the earliest references to the chest being kept in the bedchamber is also a most interesting and entertaining bit of documentation. It is found in a book of ghost stories published by Christopher Sauer in 1744. One of the tales, set in the Oley Valley of Berks County in August of the previous year, makes prominent mention of a chest. Twice, Elisabeth Yoder sees the ghost of her father and speaks with it in the *Kammer*. During the recital of the events and conversation of the second appearance of the ghost, the writer twice tells the reader that Elisabeth was sitting on the chest while she conversed with her father's spirit. The writer mentions sitting on the chest so matter-of-factly that one can easily infer that the chest was used as commonly for sitting as it was for storage. Its use in this manner would certainly explain why the lids of so many chests have been rubbed clean of paint.[43]

Much more prosaic, but slightly more informative concerning the location of chests and their contents, are the estate inventories filed in the various county courthouses of southeastern Pennsylvania. Most of these inventories, unfortunately, are running lists with no indication of what furniture was in which room. A sampling of some that do show room designations indicates chests in upper floor spaces called variously "attic," "garret," "bedroom," the "east room" of a second floor, "front room upstairs," the "north room" of a second floor, "southwest room upstairs," or merely "upstairs" or on the "second story." Chests are infrequently designated as being on the first floors of houses. More often than not just where a chest stood can only be guessed by considering the items of furniture listed around it. Most of the time the chest will be found listed just before or after a "bed and bedstead."

Chests are sometimes listed with other furnishings that are evidently in kitchens or outbuildings. These chests—in working spaces—probably did not contain clothing or bed linens. In the inventory of Caspar Moyer (Worcester Township, Montgomery County, 1792) a chest in the kitchen held lumber and shoemaker's tools. Conrad Rösli (Lower Saucon Township, Northampton County, 1794) had a "chest with some dried apples" listed after some wagons and bags and just before a saddle. Presumably this was in an outbuilding, for, following a listing of a table and chairs, Rösli also is seen to have owned a "Chest," a "German Chest and a Small Chest," and a "Chest and a Dow drauff [dough trough]." The item following these in the list was a kitchen dresser.

Inventories of the contents of chests are even harder to locate. When they do come to light, they often appear in a manner similar to the following: "Sundry wearing apparel in a large chest" (Inventory of Rebecca Brodhead, Berks County, 1788); "To a chest with linnen" (Elizabeth Wentz, Worcester Township, Montgomery County, 1789); "A black walnut chest and all the linnen and sheets" (Abraham Moyer, Providence Township, Montgomery County, 1794); "a chest with bedings" (Abraham Yotter, Upper Hanover Township, Montgomery County, 1836).

Clothing and bedding were folded and laid flat in the chests proper and in any drawers at the bottom. Many times, though, some things were also suspended in the chest. More than a few Pennsylvania-German chests have two tacks or short nails hammered into the underside of the lid—one at either end and about at the axis of the long dimension. Some of these pairs of tacks still have attached to them a slightly-slack length of string or twine. Whatever was hung from this string must have been quite pliable for it would have folded down upon itself when the lid was lowered. It is thought that stockings were hung there.

That money was also kept in the chests—possibly in the till as is said to have been the tradition in Europe—is evident from these three citations, also from estate inventories: "Cash found in the chest of the deceased 10-5-?" (Henry Smith, Frederick Township, Montgomery County, 1793); "Cash in her chest 4-16-0" (Barbara Jacobs, Skippack Township, Montgomery County, 1788); "Cash in her chest in paper money 7-0-0" (Veronica Dodderer, Frederick Township, Philadelphia County, 1752).[44]

The inner surface of the lid of the chest was sometimes used as a "picture frame." In the eighteenth and early nineteenth centuries, when very few framed items hung on the walls of rural Pennsylvania-German homes, decorated paper was often exhibited on the underside of a chest lid. These paper items—if not added recently to deceive a prospective purchaser of the chest—most likely belonged to the original owners. Most often, however, when the lid of an antique chest is lifted, merely bare planed wood is found with no trace of any appliqués. A surprising number of times the underside of the lid will exhibit the telltale traces of decorated paper that has been removed. It was once a common practice, in fact, for dealers or collectors to remove with difficulty a fraktur from a chest that was "otherwise of no interest." Occasionally, however, the underside of a lid will still have glued on it a small fancy picture, a birth certificate, or perhaps even a series of manuscript decorations lovingly placed there shortly after the chest was made. Where possible, these paper items deserve to stay exactly where their owners put them. They are as much a part of the history of the chest as any external decoration.

Cabinetmaking and Woods

Little is known about the training of the cabinetmakers who worked in rural Pennsylvania in the eighteenth century. The furniture itself provides the best evidence that some of the earlier craftsmen had received formal training in Europe. This visual evidence is buttressed by occasional entries in records which indicate the occupation of an immigrant.[45] More than a few craftsmen who had European training and who arrived penniless on the Philadelphia docks must have been apprenticed for a time to cabinetmakers in that city or in Lancaster. Most who worked in Pennsylvania, however, were born there and were probably trained by an older generation of craftsmen.

The rigorous control of the craftsmen by guilds, common in Europe, did not exist in Pennsylvania. This situation was commented upon by Gottlieb Mittelberger, an immigrant who arrived there in 1750 and returned to Europe four years later.

> No trade or profession in Pennsylvania is bound by guilds; every one may carry on whatever business he will or can, and if any one can or would carry on ten trades, no one would have a right to prevent him; and if, for instance, a lad as an apprentice, or through his own unaided exertions, learns his art or trade in six months, he can pass for a master, and may marry whenever he chooses.[46]

Written, as it is, in a book that attempts to discourage further immigration to America, this observation cannot be taken completely at face value. Yet, the comment is still a valuable observation of the work situation in the colonies. Although there were systems of apprenticeship being practiced on this side of the Atlantic, the limiting rules and regulations of the ancient European guilds were not in force. Craftsmen were freer to practice their crafts as they saw fit, but the best of them almost certainly served an exacting period of apprenticeship with an older master.

Although furniture by eighteenth- and early nineteenth-century Pennsylvania-German cabinetmakers is plentiful, documentation is rare. Available, however, are a handful of account books kept by some of the early craftsmen which provide details of how and when they worked. One such book, used by Abraham Overholt of Bedminster Township, Bucks County, contains entries from at least as early as 1791 until 1833. Overholt lists ten chests among the pieces of furniture made for local customers. All were made between 1791 and 1799 and ranged in price from £0.10.4 for a "walnut chest" to £3.0.0 for a "walnut chest with three drawers, locks and hardware." Overholt made poplar chests for £1.12.0 and £1.17.6. The first had two drawers and was painted red; the second had three drawers and was "blue speckled." A pine chest with three drawers was painted brown and cost the customer £1.10.0. Although he worked at least until 1833, Overholt lists no more sales of chests after 1799. He does, however, list chests of drawers, the most expensive of which sold for £7.10.0.[47]

Judging from the accounts of cabinetmakers such as Abraham Overholt and Peter Rank, the output of chests by any one craftsman during his working years could be relatively small. An examination of the various tax lists of the late eighteenth and early nineteenth centuries points up the fact that woodworkers seem never to have been in short supply in southeastern Pennsylvania. Customers for them seem also not to have been lacking.

Cabinetmakers such as Overholt and his contemporaries worked with a selection of tools—planes, chisels, saws, bits and braces—that had changed little in form since Roman times.[48] Some of the tools used in Pennsylvania would almost certainly have been imported, but others could easily have been made by the local blacksmith.

Possessing training and tools, craftsmen had no problem in obtaining the lumber for making chests. At least during the eighteenth century, Pennsylvania was covered with virgin forests from which a variety of woods were obtainable. Although no comprehensive program of microanalysis has been undertaken of any representative group of Pennsylvania-German chests, it is clear that the favorite wood of the country cabinetmaker was the so-called "tulip poplar." This tree (*Liriodendron tulipifera*) is actually a species of magnolia and is unrelated to the trees of the genus *Populus*. The tulip tree grew in great abundance and sometimes reached a height of over 100 feet with a diameter of 6 feet.[49] True poplar was also frequently used in Pennsylvania furniture. This was timber cut probably from stands of the eastern cottonwood (*Populus deltoides*). The two woods can be found combined in the same piece of furniture with various species of pine, chestnut, and even oak or walnut. Of course, if the piece was painted, the mismatched wood colors and grains made little difference.

The eastern black walnut (*Juglans nigra*) was also readily available to the cabinetmakers in stands of sizeable trees.[50] Given its availability and its beauty when properly finished, it is surprising that it is not found more often than it is in Pennsylvania-German chests. But among the rural customers, natural walnut was definitely a second choice to painted wood. This fact, in itself, is an indication of the prevalence of southern-German taste and tradition in Pennsylvania. When, however, walnut *was* used as the principal wood in a chest, it was finished off to bring out the beauty of its color and grain, and was thus almost never painted. Although several walnut chests have been found which have some motifs painted on the natural finish (Fig. 137), they are most often decorated only with inlays of contrasting wood or of sulfur.

Except in one or two chests from the middle of the eighteenth century (Figs. 53 and 201), oak seems not to have been used by Pennsylvania-German cabinetmakers to any appreciable extent. Harder to work and not a wood favored by southern-German craftsmen, it was passed over in favor of the softer tulip wood, poplar, and pine.

Construction

At its simplest, the Pennsylvania-German chest is a rectangular box with flat-planed boards for each of the six surfaces, comprised of the top, the bottom, the two ends, the front and the back. All six boards are quite frequently each of one piece. When enough wide timber was not handy, the cabinetmakers resorted to gluing and to tongue-and-groove construction, as did their European counterparts. The plank thickness favored by the cabinetmaker was $1^{3}/_{16}$ inches or $^{7}/_{8}$ inches.

The body of the chest is virtually always joined at the four corners by standard dovetailing. The boards are cut so that the fishtail or birdtail configuration of each dovetail lies on the front and back surfaces of the chest. The rectangular configuration thus can be seen only on the ends of the chest. The depth of the dovetail into the sides or front or back of the chest is determined by the thickness of the plank used. The angle or wedge side of the dovetail, however, was determined by the pattern used by the individual cabinetmaker. Dealers and collectors of Pennsylvania furniture frequently state that the dovetails on early chests are smaller than they are on later chests. Then again, these same informants sometimes say—with full sincerity—that just the reverse is true—that, on the early chests, the dovetails are larger than they are on the later ones. There is no rule of thumb that can be trusted. A number of measurements of the dovetails on dated pieces have been taken. The conclusion is that there is no correlation between date of chest and size of dovetail.

The overall sizes of Pennsylvania-German chests stay within surprisingly fixed limits. Chests from the period circa 1765 to circa 1820 are generally found to measure between $20 \times 47\frac{3}{8} \times 21\frac{1}{4}$ inches and $26\frac{1}{2} \times 51 \times 24$ inches if they are without drawers, and $21\frac{3}{4} \times 41 \times 18\frac{1}{4}$ inches and $31\frac{1}{2} \times 54 \times 24$ inches if drawers are included. Naturally, any combination of the measurements within the limits given is possible on any one piece of furniture.

Chests are frequently found with a rank of drawers below the large box of the chest proper. Two drawers of equal size or two drawers of equal size flanking a smaller drawer are the most common arrangements. One decorated chest has only one long drawer across the bottom of the chest. When a chest is constructed with drawers, it then has two "bottoms." The first is placed into the sides and the front and back of the chest above the level of the top of the drawer sides. The dowels which hold it in place are usually masked on the outside of the chest by a narrow applied molding. This molding is usually found on the front and on both ends of the chest, but sometimes on the front only. The true bottom of the chest is situated just under the drawers.

On a relatively small number of chests, the bottom boards have been extended slightly beyond the front and ends and filed to form a false molding (Figs. 53 and 54). The back of the bottom boards is, as usual, flush with the backboard of the chest. This peculiar detail is so seldom seen that it has so far been impossible to determine how widely it was in use in Pennsylvania cabinetmaking.

On a very small number of chests, the bottom section housing the drawers has been stepped out from the sides of the other portion of the chest (Figs. 14 and 215). This is a method of construction apparently not found in German chests of the eighteenth century, but it is utilized in English cabinetwork of the same period.

The drawers themselves are of simple five-piece construction. The sides are generally attached to the fronts by dovetailing in the better-made chests. In many, the backs and bottoms are doweled or nailed. As a rule, the drawer fronts of the earlier chests have a molded lip. In nineteenth-century chests this drawer front is generally flat or rounded and may fit flush against the face of the chest.

A small built-in container, or till, is almost always found inside chests. Usually this is mounted on the left side, but it is also occasionally found on the right. This small storage area is found inside German chests dating from as early as the end of the fifteenth century and is known in German as a *Deckelkästchen, Beilade*, or even as a *Lade in der Lade*. It is thought that it originally may have been intended for the storage of jewels or other small items of adornment.[51]

In Pennsylvania chests the till is more often than not constructed of two boards about ⅝ inches thick set into the sides and end of the chest at right angles. The lid is made of another rectangular board, also set into the sides by means of two dowels on which it can be made to pivot. By this method, it is opened and closed. The till lid, when opened, swings up. Scratch marks on the underside of chest lids themselves indicate that the till top has often been used as a device to prop open the larger lid. Sometimes there will be one, two, or three smaller drawers set into the bottom section of the till. The till may also be found with a false front that lifts to reveal a hidden drawer. These drawers are almost all concealed in the same manner, so that they are hardly ever really "secret." On the average the till is about 5 inches high by 18¾ inches long by 5 inches deep. The addition of drawers, secret or otherwise, adds depth to the till.

Quite a few chests survive which seem never to have had feet or supports of any kind. While it is not impossible that these chests were set directly on the floor, there may also have been supports that were not permanently attached and which have been lost. There is at least one large case piece—a walnut wardrobe in a private collection—the original two runners of which are not nailed, doweled, or otherwise joined to the bottom of the case. When the runners are properly positioned on the floor, the case is then set on them. Such detached runners could easily have been used with the smaller chests.

A number of chests survive with the original attached runners still in place (Figs. 59, 153 and 224). These runners are secured with dowels or nails, or are driven into a bottom-flared channel cut into the bottom of the chest. This latter method of attachment is exactly like that used for the battens which so often are seen on the undersides of Pennsylvania-German table tops.

Turned feet are not uncommon on Pennsylvania chests. There are almost always four, but at least one maker chose to give one of his chests five (Fig. 78). Turned feet seem to be most popular on chests from the 1760's and 1770's and then again after about 1820. The earlier feet are generally more like a disc or ball in profile than the feet of the nineteenth-century chests, which tend to have a height greater than their diameter.

. By far the most common support for the chest is the plinth or bracket-base. Made up of three or four lengths of lumber joined at the corners by dovetailing, the Pennsylvania bases are never as cumbersome as those seen on Continental chests. Here again, the more subtle detailing of English cabinetmaking seems to have left its mark in the craftsmanship of the German artisans working in rural Pennsylvania. The pronounced horizontal line of the bracket base is frequently relieved by the use of a scrolled pattern cut out of the planking.

The most elaborate foot made by the cabinetmaker was the ogee. Named for the double-curve formed by the union of a concave with a convex line, the ogee foot was a detail taken over directly from English high-style cabinetry. Carved either from a solid block of wood, or from two or more laminated pieces, it is never seen on rural chests from the Continent. It was the most difficult foot to make, and thus is not found nearly so often as the bracket foot sawed from a wooden plank.

The lid of a Pennsylvania-German chest—at least one that is decorated—is always flat, never curved, and is generally made of a single board. It is never formed with two or more panels as is so often the case with European examples (Figs. 4 and 5), nor is it ever constructed with a tray-top (Fig. 15). The end and front edges of the lid are almost always trimmed with molding applied with wooden dowels.

On some chests the front portion of the molding is doweled and the end portions are both doweled and tenoned to the lid.

From the middle of the eighteenth century onward, English style and taste in cabinetmaking influenced the Pennsylvania-German craftsman. There are, therefore, very few Pennsylvania-German chests that are a pure Germanic form. The so-called "architectural type" is the most Continental in design, but even some of them rest on the ogee feet that are certainly more English than German. The result of this obvious acculturation—the Pennsylvania German *Kischt*—is a furniture form that is neither German nor English, but a unique form that combines outstanding characteristics from the furniture craft of both cultures.

The superstructure of the "architectural chest"—the more elaborate of the two basic types of Pennsylvania-German chest—is the same as that of its simpler counterpart. It is a four-board enclosure with a lid, resting upon a plank bottom. To the front, or to the front and both ends, however, a second layer of wood has been applied. This layer is cut out or pieced together into the familiar arched top panels. Thus, the thickness of the arcaded surfaces of an architectural chest is naturally double that of the simpler chest.

Since the second layer of wood is applied to the outer surface of the superstructure, the inner walls of the chest are perfectly flat. Any chest which has panels on the inside of the chest—raised up from the flat background—is assuredly a chest that has been altered to the more uncommon, and therefore more marketable, architectural form.

The architectural chest always has three panels on the face of the chest. These panels usually are formed by combining five or more carefully cut pieces of lumber on the face of the box. The largest piece runs across the top of the front and has the arches of the panels cut into it. Four vertical rectangles are ranged under this piece to form the pilasters flanking the sunken surfaces. These pilasters are frequently molded or reeded. On some chests there may also be a long narrow member applied along the bottom of the face of the chest to define the bottom of the panels. A small piece of horizontal molding is usually attached at the top of the pilaster at the point where the arch springs. The inner curve of the arch itself is sometimes also edged with molding or, rather, has been molded with a molding plane. The ends, as well, of some of the more ambitiously constructed chests may be embellished with arched top panels.

Dated examples of the architectural chest range from 1764 to 1795. At the end of the eighteenth century, the form seems to have fallen out of favor—either because it was by that time considered old-fashioned or because a new generation of cabinetmakers chose only to work in simpler forms.

Hardware

Pennsylvania-German chests carry both iron and brass hardware, sometimes in substantial quantity on any one given chest. A fully developed chest over three drawers might have—in the way of iron—two large hinges, one large and three small locks, and two carrying handles. In brass, the same chest might have four keyhole escutcheons and five drawer pulls.

The ironwork used on the chests may have been manufactured locally or it may have been imported. Before the middle of the eighteenth century, when the first locally-made chests recorded in this study appear, domestic manufactures in Pennsylvania—including iron—were often noted in the Philadelphia press.[52] Before 1776 there were 81 ironworks in the colony[53] and in 1788 there were over 200 blacksmiths in Philadelphia alone.[54] Scores of anvils were also scattered across the countryside, many manned by smiths who worked them in addition to farming. From the middle of the century until the beginning of the Revolutionary War, Pennsylvania produced enough iron to export a considerable tonnage to the mother country.[55] Doubtless, an even greater amount was reserved for use at home for the making of the hard goods and utensils so necessary to sustain life in a rural economy.

While iron hinges and locks could certainly be obtained from local rural smiths, they could also be purchased from merchants in the larger towns and cities. In the late summer of 1755, Thomas Maal of Second Street, Philadelphia, advertised in the Germantown newspaper, along with other hardware and dry goods:

kisten-schlösser   [chest locks
handhaben und bänder   handles and hinges
H und HL bänder   H and HL hinges
schwalben schwansz-bänder   swallowtail hinges]

and noted that he also carried:

sonst allerlei messinge und eiserne bänder
[various kinds of brass and iron hinges.]

Maal's advertisement does not indicate whether the hardware was imported or made locally.[56] The important thing to note is that the types of hardware which were available could be bought from city outlets as well as from local smiths.

Hinges, of course, are the most important items of hardware on a chest since they serve to secure the lid to the box. Hinges are also usually the most easily identifiable pieces of hardware on the chests from a stylistic viewpoint. The work of one blacksmith is so frequently joined with that of the same cabinetmaker that there is good reason to suspect that much of the ironwork used on Pennsylvania-German chests was indeed of local manufacture. If the chest makers were not buying their iron from a local forge, then some of them must have worked over a long period of time with a single stock of iron purchased from a wholesaler such as Maal.

The hinges range from crude to superlative in design and execution. Fine wrought iron is one of the great glories of Pennsylvania-German decorative art. Often some of the most skillful work to go into the making of a chest may be hidden from view until the lid is lifted. More than a few chests, unadorned or chastely painted on the outside, are brilliantly decorated on the interior with hinges that blossom into iron flowers. While those hinges that actually do end in leaf and flower motifs are relatively scarce, there are many hundreds of pairs of hinges which are formed into other interesting decorative shapes. The basic form of the hinge is generally that of a long tapering triangle, elaborated with whatever shapes appealed to the smith. (Figs. 16–21.)

A hinge form that is found on chests dating from the second half of the eighteenth century and the first quarter of the nineteenth is the simple tapered shape with an inverted triangle at the tip (Fig. 22).

Since it often seems to have been cut from sheet metal rather than hammered from bar iron as were most hinges of better quality, and since it is such a ubiquitous shape, it may well be one of the more common factory-made forms.

In the second decade of the nineteenth century, the butt-hinge appears. It is attached with screws rather than round-headed nails or rivets and takes over from the earlier long hinge forms as that most widely used (Fig. 23).

Except for the mass-produced items made from sheet metal, most hinges, both simple and elaborate, were probably hammered from iron bars or rods. Rough formed under the hammer, much of the detail of the shapes was achieved by finishing with a file. The filed areas, which are found generally along the edges of a hinge, show up as bright surfaces against the black metal of the flat part. When the hinges have been protected from moisture, this contrast of bright metal against dark can be striking. The same finishing technique—accomplished by using a file—can be seen on some elements of many locks.

The upper half of any hinge on a Pennsylvania-German chest is always fastened to the underside of the lid. No Pennsylvania chest examined for this study had hinges totally on the outside as is sometimes the case with European pieces of furniture. The lower portion of the hinge is most often attached to the outside rear of the chest, but examples with the lower half on the inside of the chest are not uncommon (Fig. 25). Throughout the eighteenth century, the most common method of attaching the hinge to the chest was with round-headed rivets or with nails.

The carrying handles, which are often found attached to the ends of a chest, are always of iron. The actual handle used as a handhold is an elongated loop of metal open at one side, usually with the two ends turned upward at a ninety-degree angle so that it will act as a stop against the backplate. The backplate is either just that—a rectangular plate—or a pair of star or floral forms in iron through which the holding rings pass. The rings are generally attached to a tapered piece of iron that is hammered through the wood of the ends of the chest and clinched down inside. As the advertisement of Thomas Maal indicated, these *handhaben* or carrying handles were available commercially as early as 1755. On one chest (Fig. 116), the iron carrying handles were also mounted to serve as drawer pulls.

There are two types of locks which are found on the principal storage section of the Pennsylvania-German chest. By far the most prevalent is the crab lock. It has a spring mechanism which secures the lid of the chest by grabbing a metal drop—usually arrowhead-shaped —which is attached to the underside of the lid directly over the lock. When the key is inserted and turned, it forces the two grabbing elements of the lock aside so that the arrowhead, and thus the lid, can be raised. This type of lock is found on the majority of the chests made between the 1760's and the second decade of the nineteenth century. Many of the locks are beautifully made, with the same fine finishing details done with a file that one sees on hinges. Some of the locks are even decorated with fancy engraving (Fig. 28).

The second type of lock utilizes a sliding bar mechanism enclosed in a metal box. These locks are found on the 1741 chest at the Winterthur Museum (Fig. 200), as well as on several of the chests dating from the 1760's. It is a type also seen on at least one chest made in the 1780's (Fig. 29). These early examples have a sliding bar which passes horizontally through a "U"-shaped pin attached to the underside of the lid.

In the nineteenth century another type of the box lock superceded the crab lock as the favored form. This new type works on a slightly different principle: the chest is secured by the bar sliding vertically into a metal-lined hole in the lid. These later locks are generally not so heavy as the earlier locks of the same type.

It is well to remember that Pennsylvania-German craftsmen may have sometimes reused hardware from earlier furniture. Their conservatism also kept old styles alive for a long time after they were outmoded in the city. Consequently, one should resist the temptation to generalize about hardware when dating a chest. If the piece of furniture is not clearly dated in paint or inlay, the style of lock or hinges may not be *the* clue that will give the desired information.

The locks on the drawers in the lower section of a chest always have a vertically sliding bar. Frequently the bar does not slide up into a metal opening, as is the case with some of the larger locks, but only into a hole cut into the wood framing above the drawer. Set into the backs of the drawer fronts, these small locks are usually fastened to the wood with screws.

An iron guard may also be found around the keyhole. Some are very simple ovals or rectangles, but many reveal touches of country Baroque detail, delightful in their playfulness. Some of the finer of these guards or escutcheons will even have a protruding edge around the keyhole to guide the key into place (Fig. 31).

It has not been possible to ascertain if keys were cast in Pennsylvania or were only imported. Henry Kauffman finds no evidence that any "fine" keys were made here,[57] but simple keys of the type used with the chest locks could conceivably have been forged and filed by Pennsylvania locksmiths at an early date. Considering the high quality of other ironwork attributed to such craftsmen, the problems of key-making should hardly have been insurmountable.

Rarely is the hardware on chests signed. Markings, when they are found, are in the form of either initials or names of makers—on both hinges and locks. At least one pair of hinges (Fig. 33) bears what are probably the blacksmith's initials on the right-hand hinge and the date of manufacture on the left. Locks are more frequently found with markings than hinges. Both initials and die-stamped names have been observed (Fig. 35). The large "N" which is frequently found on the top surface of crab locks is almost certainly not a maker's initial, but rather a space-filling device. This "N" appears on locks attached to chests from the entire southeastern Pennsylvania area and over a period of at least forty years (1770–1810). It is most unlikely that one maker is responsible for all these locks so marked or that all the makers had the same initial. The use of the "N" is probably a retention of the practice followed by European lock makers.

While it is possible to find chest drawers that appear never to have had hardware of any kind, most carry brass pulls and keyhole plates. As noted, as many as nine pieces of brass—sometimes not all of matching design—can be found on a three-drawer chest. The earliest native chest examined—one at Winterthur dated 1741—bears four matching engraved rococo brass pulls on its two drawers (Fig. 200). A chest with two drawers and a full complement of four pulls and two keyhole plates can be found as early as 1763.

These decorative brasses were available to Pennsylvania craftsmen at a relatively early date. In 1718 the inventory of one Chester "joyner," Robert Streater, listed "Small locks & some drop Souchins [escutcheons with tear-shaped drops attached]," both items almost certainly imported.[58] John Stow, brass founder in Philadelphia, reported as early as August 3, 1749, however, that "he makes and sells all manner of brass work," but he made no direct reference to hardware for furniture.[59] At least one brass drawer pull with his name has been discovered, so it is not impossible that he both imported and made furniture hardware. Merchants in Philadelphia had advertised furniture fittings before 1749. In 1727, Francis Richardson advertised that he had "escutchins" in his Market Street shop,[60] and in the Spring of 1749 another Philadelphia joiner advertised hardware, specifying that it was imported.[61]

The imported hardware used in Philadelphia was of English manufacture. The importation would almost certainly have been drastically limited, if not completely stopped, by the ban placed on British imports by the Continental Association in 1774. The resolution encouraging the ban was passed by the First Continental Congress on October 20, 1774, and the non-importation policy went into effect on December 1. The Pennsylvania Assembly approved the edict against importation, and committees were organized to enforce it in eight of the ten counties of the Commonwealth by February 5, 1775. By the beginning of February all ships bearing imports from England or Ireland were prevented from unloading at Philadelphia.[62]

In August of 1783, a month before the formal end of hostilities, at least one Philadelphia merchant, Samuel Rowland Fisher of the firm of Joshua Fisher & Son, traveled to England to make contact again with manufacturers who could supply goods for business in America. An English catalogue containing 146 pages of engraved plates depicting furniture hardware which was used by Fisher is now in the collection at Winterthur. The name of the manufacturer who issued the catalogue is not known, but because of the watermarks on the paper and the dates of Fisher's trips to England, it can be dated to the period 1776–1789. The catalogue was presumably acquired by him between 1783 and 1789, possibly on his first postwar trip.[63]

Many of the plates show pulls and keyhole plates like those seen on Pennsylvania-German chests (Figs. 37 and 38). There is certainly no reason to doubt that the rural Pennsylvania-German craftsmen obtained their hardware from this same source—the English manufacturer. Imported and handled by the merchants of Philadelphia, this hardware would easily have found its way inland to smaller dealers and to the craftsmen themselves. While the brasses would not have been imported during the Revolutionary War, it is obvious that a good supply was held on hand by the country cabinetmakers. Brass does not seem to be lacking on any of the chests dated during the war years.

Brass plates with bails are attached to the drawer fronts by pairs of combination bailholder-screws (Fig. 39). Square nuts hold the two screws in place and the brass plate flat against the front of the drawer. When some of the brasses are removed, it is very easy to see that the hardware was sometimes attached while the paint on the chest was still wet. Brasses without bails are generally attached to the wood with roundheaded nails. Frequently, the back of the drawer front was cut out around the holes drilled for the screws so that the nut lay below the surface of the inside of the drawer.

The traffic in English brasses of the styles so familiar to us here seems not to have extended to mainland Europe. The typical brass pull or keyhole plate in the so-called "Chippendale" style has not been observed on any of the chests known to have been made in rural Germany or Switzerland. In Scandinavia, however, they are sometimes found on painted chests of drawers.

As tastes changed in American cities at the turn of the eighteenth century, more and different hardware became available from both domestic and foreign sources. Throughout the nineteenth century the country cabinetmakers of Pennsylvania strove to keep up with the times—at least in regard to hardware. The chests they were making might be hopelessly old-fashioned by Philadelphia standards, but the attractive hardware they were using was frequently quite up-to-date. When pressed metal pulls and knobs with embossed decoration were available in city shops, they soon appeared in the rural areas. Chests made during this later period are found not only with these embossed brasses, but with solid brass knobs of diminutive size, pressed glass knobs, and even—late in the century—with white porcelain knobs of the kind usually associated with the most utilitarian furniture such as kitchen cabinets and tool chests. Obviously, as the importance of the chest declined in the Pennsylvania-German household, the quality of the hardware deteriorated noticeably.

Surface Decoration

The three forms of surface decoration used by Pennsylvania-German cabinetmakers were carving, inlay, and painting. Of all the chests examined during the course of research for this book, only one had any carved decoration. Even here, the carving was minimal and consisted only of a small oval cartouche on the lid. The cartouche contained script initials—evidently of the first owner of the chest.

A little shallow carving can be found on several large case pieces by Pennsylvania-German craftsmen (notably the Herr wardrobe at Winterthur and the Huber wardrobe in the Philadelphia Museum of Art), but the use of the technique is certainly far from commonplace. Two reasons can be given for the absence of carving from the craft techniques of rural Pennsylvania. The first is the ingrained tradition of the furniture makers of southern Germany. As noted, the south of Germany was mainly an area of painted rather than carved furniture. The second reason easily follows from the first. Those who became cabinetmakers in Pennsylvania's rural areas during the period the decorated chest was most popular probably did not receive any training in carving while apprentices. In addition, rural customers evidently did not demand carving on their furniture.

One type of carving—careful gouging, really—was skillfully practiced in Pennsylvania by those who decorated furniture with inlay. It was, however, the simplest kind of chisel-work, being little more than the removal of a shallow depth of wood between carefully plotted lines.

With one exception all the inlaid chests examined have been of walnut. This one exception is of quarter-sawed sycamore (Fig. 116). In this chest the wood inlaid into the surface is a light-colored wood as in the walnut chests. This, indeed, is almost always the case with Pennsylvania-German inlaid furniture, but pewter and a substance heretofore considered "white wax" are also found. Without exhaustive wood analysis, which would of necessity destroy portions of the inlays, it is impossible to identify exactly what woods were most commonly used for this purpose. American holly (*Ilex opaca*) was evidently widely used, and the timbers are said even to have been imported to Europe for use in cabinetwork.[64] Charles Montgomery, in his study of American Federal furniture in the Winterthur collection, concludes that "In urban centers holly was the wood most widely used for stringing," but "In the country, maple and birch were often substituted."[65] Stringing is the type of inlay in which long narrow strips of filler material are used in the darker wood.

Pewter was used by only a handful of Pennsylvania-German cabinetmakers. It was employed alone in several wardrobes as the material for the inlay, and in at least one instance was combined with wood inlay in a chest of walnut (Fig. 76).

The most unusual type of Pennsylvania-German furniture decoration is that utilizing sulfur inlay which was formerly believed to have been executed with a compound of white lead and beeswax.[66] Recent laboratory tests on six pieces of furniture from both institutional and private collections have shown that the inlay material is not any compound, but is indeed sulfur. It is clear from a close examination of the channels prepared in the wood for the sulfur that it was introduced in a molten state. It not only filled the channels, but also penetrated into the wood grain. After it had solidified it was then polished off level with the surface of the wood.

Equally as handsome as the more conventional wood inlay, sulfur inlay must have been much faster and easier to execute. The craftsman was spared hours of tedious work by not having to cut the tiny pieces of inlay to fit the channels he had prepared for his design. The technique may have been improvised by an enterprising Pennsylvania cabinetmaker, for no prototype of this kind of decoration has thus far been located in Europe.

Of the twenty-two pieces of furniture so far recorded with sulfur inlay, all are of walnut. Nine of the pieces are chests. They range in date from 1765 to the middle of the last decade of the eighteenth century. All seem to have been made not too far from the city of Lancaster.[67]

Paint

Protective coats of varnish or shellac were certainly used by some rural Pennsylvania craftsmen on the completed chests. Those made of walnut were probably always varnished to protect the surface of the wood and bring out the color and the grain. Except in rare cases, the chests constructed of soft woods were given a coat of paint. Even a cursory look at the American furniture of the seventeenth, eighteenth, and early nineteenth centuries will indicate that paint was the finish most in use. It could be both a preservative and a decorative element. As a preservative, paint was used from the time of the earliest settlement of America by Europeans. The oldest known piece of painted American furniture is a chest thought to have been made either in Portsmouth, New Hampshire, or Ipswich, Massachusetts, in the period 1660 to 1680.[68] Paint was also certainly used in Pennsylvania from the beginning of European settlement in the seventeenth century.

Pennsylvania has mineral pigment deposits of ochre, umber, sienna, iron ore, and black, yellow, and red shales in a number of places in Northampton, Lehigh, Berks, Lancaster, York, and Adams counties. While it is possible that some of these deposits were worked in the colonial era,[69] most of the pigments used for the making of paints in Pennsylvania in the eighteenth century were almost certainly imported through Philadelphia and other eastern seaports.[70] These same pigments, and the vehicles with which they were mixed, would have been used by all practitioners of the craft of painting—furniture decorators as well as the painters of house interiors and exteriors.

Advertisements for pigments, oils, and painters' materials can be found in American newpapers throughout the eighteenth century. Philadelphia, as the largest city in the colonies, was certainly the main supply point for all of Pennsylvania. Christopher Marshall, "next door to the Bird in Hand," advertised as "just imported" a selection of colors in 1741.[71] Six years later another Philadelphia merchant advertised a list of approximately forty pigments.[72] Thus, it is evident that a wide selection of color was available commercially at a fairly early date, even in the interior of Pennsylvania. On March 29, 1764, close to the time of the making of the first painted chests studied for this publication, the *Pennsylvania Journal* printed an advertisement for the Lancaster druggist James Peters. After a lengthy recital of the drugs imported "in the last vessels at Philadelphia from London," and a note on the availability of "medicine chests and boxes from £3. to £50.," is a postscript of special interest:

> All sorts of colours neatly prepared either for house of [sic] face painting *viz*. White lead ground in oil, red lead, oaker [,] umber. Spanish brown, Prussian blue. verdegrease, lampblack [,] ivory black, linseed oil, nut oil, oil of turpentine, boiled oil [,] leaf gold and silver, blue smalts, carmine, ultramine [sic] vermillion [,] drop lake, flake white, Indian ink, together, with brushes, camel hair pencils, gally-pots, bottles, viols, sieves, mortars, instruments, &c.

White lead was a basic lead carbonate that was generally bright white, unless contaminated. It was one of the most important imported pigments available to the painter in the eighteenth century and was used as a putty, primer, and base color. The first organized factory in America for the manufacture of white lead was not opened until 1804 by Samuel Wetherill in Philadelphia. Flake white was held to be the best grade of white available in the eighteenth century by some observers. Others did not believe that it was any better than other whites. There is also some confusion as to how it was made, but the basic material was lead.

Three reds were available to James Peters' customers in 1764. Red lead was not very often used as a pigment, but rather as a priming material or as a ground for more brilliant reds. It also served as a flux in the manufacture of glass. Spanish brown can actually be considered as a red, being a coarse ochre that occurred in deposits in several parts of England, but it was also imported from the Continent. It was used chiefly for grounds and priming by house painters. Vermilion is a compound formed of sulfur and mercury. Although manufacture of this pigment is said to have begun in England shortly after the middle of the eighteenth century, Holland was almost certainly the source of supply for that sold by Peters. Records show that just under 32,000 pounds were imported into England in 1760.[73] Its manufacture was extremely dangerous because of the mercury vapor produced during the process.

The discovery of Prussian blue was announced by the Berlin Academy in 1710, hence the name. It was an excellent pigment and worked well with oil and with distemper. It could not be used with casein paints or whitewash, however, since lime destroyed the color. Smalt was made by vitrifying a mixture of calcined cobalt ore and pulverized flint. Rather coarse, it was sometimes actually scattered dry on a tacky paint base and evened out with a feather. Ultramarine was made from lapis lazuli. It was a bright blue and very tedious to make because of the fine grinding necessary. It was therefore a very expensive pigment when made from the natural mineral, and it is doubtful if it was ever used for covering large areas such as the boards of a chest. Artificial ultramarine was accidentally discovered in France in 1814 and the pigment, consequently, became cheaper and more widely used.

Until late in the eighteenth century there were very few green pigments available, and James Peters could offer only "verdegrease." Verdigrise was made by corroding copper with acetic acid. During the second half of the eighteenth century and the first half of the nineteenth, Montpelier, France, was one of the principal centers for its manufacture. The pigment was poisonous, but not as deadly as any of the arsenic-based greens which came late in the eighteenth century. A more refined verdigrise was also made by dissolving the pigment in rectified vinegar. The fine deep blue-green color which resulted was a pigment that often turned black with time. This, of course, is a condition that is often noted by the careful observer of Pennsylvania-German furniture—a green or blue background that has turned almost black—and may be the result of using this pigment.

"Oaker" would probably have been brown ochre, an iron oxide pigment that was available in a range of colors from brown through orange. Umber was a very stable brown ochre. In its raw state it was light brown in color. When burned, it took on a warmer reddish-brown color.

The Peters advertisement lists both lampblack and ivory black. Both were common pigments composed of pure carbon. Lampblack was made by burning resins or oils or other materials in a closed space. The resultant soot was scraped and used as a pigment. Ivory black was made by soaking chips of ivory in linseed oil and baking them until they were black coals. It was much more expensive than lampblack.

Both "drop lake" and carmine would have been red pigments made by precipitating cochineal, Brazilwood, or the red dye extracted from scarlet rags on an earth base such as alumina or chalk or cuttlefish bone. The colors tended to become transparent when wet with oil, so were seldom used in that medium except as glazing colors. "Drop lake" was one of the better lakes which had been pressed through a funnel when semi-dry. As it dried it formed large drops or cones and was merchandised in that manner. Carmine was formed directly from cochineal, a dye prepared from an insect found in Latin America and the West Indies which was dried for its coloring matter. It supposedly took 70,000 insects to make a pound of carmine.[74] Understandably a very expensive color and considered the finest of the red lake pigments, carmine did not mix well with oil. Since it worked well with water, Peters may have sold it for use in making red ink.

With the exception of a good yellow, all the colors that would be necessary to complete the most complicated palette of the eighteenth-century Pennsylvania-German decorator were available from James Peters in 1764. In Philadelphia, the source of supply for Peters, this other color would almost certainly have been in the stock of one of the importers at some time or other. The pigment might have been either the earths, yellow ochre or raw sienna, or massicot, a lead-tin yellow, which was more popular in the seventeenth century than in the eighteenth.[75] Patent yellow, so called because of an English patent for its manufacture held by one James Turner and dated February 1781, was popular during the last decade of the century and even after the introduction of chrome yellow in the nineteenth.[76] It, or some other pigment designated "patent yellow," was advertised for sale in Philadelphia by John M'Elwee, glazier, as early as 1789.[77]

As new pigments were perfected they could have appeared in Pennsylvania within months of their commercial availability in London. Cobalt blue was discovered in 1802 and was introduced into England around 1816.[78] Emerald green was first produced commercially in Germany in 1814, as Brunswick green had been about ten years before.[79] American chrome ore had been sent to England as early as 1816 and made into pigment.[80] Some of it must have returned via paint wholesalers in Philadelphia. Cadmium yellow, however, was not available commercially until the late 1840's.[81] Whatever the case, the range of colors available to the decorator in Pennsylvania was expanded as time went by. Many came into use just as the "classic" mode of Germanic decoration was going out of fashion in rural Pennsylvania.

Ready-mixed paints were generally not available until the second half of the nineteenth century. Throughout the entire time that furniture was being elaborately decorated in rural Pennsylvania, pigments and oils would have been purchased by the prospective painter and mixed together as they were needed. Because of the formation of oil film and the separation of pigment from vehicle, it was not practical to store mixed paint. Consequently, the careful craftsman mixed only the amount that was needed to do one day's work. Some pigment, such as the white lead ground in oil advertised by James Peters, would have been wet and out of necessity would have been marketed in small crocks or bladders. The other pigments were sold dry in various degrees of fineness, and some certainly had to be reground by the buyer if any quality painting was to be done.

The assumption is made here that oil was the principal vehicle used by Pennsylvania-German painters of furniture, but this may not have been the case. Unless chemical analysis can be undertaken on selected paint samples from a representative number of Pennsylvania-German chests, there is no certainty as to just what medium was really in vogue. Gislind Ritz, one of the foremost authorities on European painted furniture, has deduced that "painting in casein is the elementary peasant technique." She also states that the oil technique did not begin to be widespread in the southern German lands until the last third of the eighteenth century. Along with these two techniques, she finds rural craftsmen painting with egg, paste, and also with size as media.[82]

If casein, however, was a common technique in rural Pennsylvania at the end of the eighteenth century, why would a recipe for a milk-base paint be introduced as a novelty in 1819? In that year, Johann Krauss had published, in Allentown, a compilation of recipes and formulae for household use, the *Oeconomisches Haus-und Kunst-Buch*.[83] Item number 339 in the book is called "*Von der Malery mit*

Milch" (painting with milk) and the formula is introduced with the comment,

> Herr Cadet-de-Vaux, ein Franzose, hat schon vor mehrern Jahren eine besondere ökonomische Methode mit Milch zu malen bekannt gemacht.
> [Herr Cadet-de-Vaux, a Frenchman, some years ago made known a particularly economical method of painting with milk.]

During the French Revolution, when linseed oil was scarce in France, Cadet-de-Vaux evolved his recipe for milk-base paint. This recipe was first published in English in the 1801 edition of *The Repertory of Arts and Manufactures*.[84] Krauss must have gotten the Cadet-de-Vaux recipe either first- or second-hand from the English publication. One can only conclude that either casein had not been a common technique in Pennsylvania or that it had been superceded for so long by the oil technique that it was indeed a novelty in 1819.

Pennsylvania-German chests were probably decorated in the shop where they were made. If not decorated by the cabinetmaker himself, they were likely painted by another member of the family. The latter practice would not have been without precedent among Germanic craftsmen, for furniture-making families, in which the men made the furniture and the women decorated it, were at work in central Europe well into the nineteenth century.[85]

Abraham Overholt, a probably not untypical cabinetmaker of Bucks County, painted chests with both solid colors and possibly textured finishes. Peter Rank of Lebanon County, who signed chests he had painted with floral decorations, also mentions in his account book that he painted such a chest. While further documentary proof would certainly be welcome, there is no reason to doubt that—in the majority of cases—all the work of construction and decoration was accomplished in the same workshop.

After smoothing the surfaces of the assembled chest, the craftsman began preparations for painting it. The paint was undoubtedly applied in the usual manner, with a brush. If the chest was to be only one color, that color was applied and the chest was left to dry. If the chest was to be grained or textured, a second coat of paint was applied over the first. Ordinarily the first coat would be the lighter of the two. The texturing itself was a removal process in which some of the dark paint from the second coat was removed to expose the lighter paint of the undercoat. From the physical evidence it is clear that the decorators used any manner of materials to work the paint. A dry stiff-bristled brush, rolled paper or cloth, corn cobs, and even feathers were utilized. In the nineteenth century, and possibly also in the eighteenth, some decorators had sets of combs made of metal or leather or other hard material with which to "comb" the wet paint into patterns.

Decoration and Decorators

Many chests were painted only one color or were covered with simple two-toned graining. Hundreds, however, were decorated with a wide variety of motifs. The simplicity or the elaborateness of these designs depended only upon the artistic ability or the ambition of the painter. It is these decorated chests that are one of the great glories of Pennsylvania-German art. They exhibit a full range of celestial and earthly subjects. Stars and birds, both identifiable and unrecognizable, are seen along with the plump heart so ubiquitous throughout rural Pennsylvania crafts. Painted blooms from gardens, both real and imagined, share space with stylish ladies and with men on horseback. Rearing lions and unicorns appear fairly often. The common house cat and the elusive mermaid are seen just one time.

The intent of the decorator in applying particular motifs is never clear. There is much conjecture as to the "meaning" of all the motifs as they are used in Pennsylvania-German art. Almost never are we given any clue by the painter himself. There are hints to be found, however, in the verbal tradition of the culture and in other items of the decorative arts from the period in which the chests were produced. With caution, we can interpolate some meaning into the more unusual motifs to be found on chests when we compare them with the same representations on other artifacts of the period. The motifs of the toasting couple, the unicorn, along with equestrian figures and the mermaid are the easiest to compare in this manner.

Rare on Pennsylvania furniture and perhaps unique to the work of one upper Berks County painter (Fig. 66), figures of a man with a drinking vessel and a woman with a flower or bouquet are common on German enameled glass of the seventeenth and eighteenth centuries (Fig. 67). On the glassware the figures are clearly emblematic of domesticity and hospitality. Often, the two figures depicted are the heads of a household, and with them will be found representations of all their children. The idea of domesticity would be an appropriate one to relate to the appearance of this motif on a chest. The woman with flowers and the man with a wine glass is also seen on a few Pennsylvania birth and baptismal certificates of the second half of the eighteenth century. Here the figures may represent the baptismal sponsors of the infant for whom the certificate was prepared.

The unicorn has intrigued students of Pennsylvania-German art as it has many others through the ages. When considering it, one must remember that to many people living in the eighteenth century the unicorn was not merely a mythical animal and a "symbol"; it was very real.[86] Although thousands in the Old World believed in the existence of the unicorn, its image is rarer in the rural arts of Germanic Europe than it is in the arts of rural Pennsylvania. Only four examples were noted in a survey of the major folk museum collections in Alsace, Germany, and Switzerland, and in only two cases was the unicorn found pictured on chests. One was on an inlaid chest in the Schweizerisches Landesmuseum in Zurich (Fig. 92) and the other is in the Rätisches Museum in Chur, also in Switzerland. The unicorn is also twice found painted on objects made in the Alpachtal of the Tirol. One time (Fig. 93) the animal is part of a procession around the sides of a small wooden box, and the other it is included in a similar procession across the front of a *Schrank* (in the Bayrisches Nationalmuseum, Munich). Both painted objects may be by the same hand. Only one time do the Old-World unicorns appear in a pair as they are so often seen in Pennsylvania. The confronted beasts were carved as part of the crowded composition on a mangel dated 1737 (Fig. 94).[87]

While tales of the unicorn could easily have been transported from Germany to America in the folkloric baggage of the immigrants, the immediate source of the motif itself is closer to home. Both the British coat-of-arms and that of the Commonwealth of Pennsylvania appear to have been an inspiration to the country decorators. That the British arms was an influence as late as 1796 can be seen on the chest decorated for Maria Grim (Fig. 132). Here the center panel contains two confronted black unicorns while the flanking panels have confronted lions supporting a crown on a tulip stalk. What we have are the two supporters of the British coat-of-arms rearranged to suit the taste of the rural Pennsylvania artist. Asymmetry was anathema to him, and, a copyist though the artist might be, the lion balanced off against a unicorn offended him—more for aesthetic reasons than political. The unicorn on the Pennsylvania chests was almost always painted wearing a collar and frequently is chained. Both are details found on the British coat-of-arms (Fig. 95).

The collar and chain on the British unicorn is very similar to the harness and reins of the horses on the Commonwealth of Pennsylvania arms (Fig. 96). These horses first appeared as supporters of the coat-of-arms of Pennsylvania when it was engraved by Caleb Lownes of Philadelphia in 1778.[88] Since the earliest dated unicorn chest is from that same year, it is tempting to see the design by Lownes as the direct source for the confronted beasts on the chests.

The motif of the horse and rider is frequently associated with that of the unicorn. In European rural arts, this motif is often evocative of the military life or a famed political leader. Frederick the Great of Prussia seems especially to have captured the fancy of the common people, and he appears in many art forms. On a ceramic piece from about the middle of the eighteenth century he is both pictorially represented and is referred to as *Alte Fritze* in the inscription (Fig. 97).

Although we often like to imagine that all the immigrants fled Europe loathing the nobility, this was not always the case. Figures clearly identified as royalty do appear in Pennsylvania-German art without any apparent derisive intent. Since Frederick the Great became a great hero in England after the Convention of Westminster in 1756 and mottoes such as "Success to the King of Prussia" were even embossed on tableware, it is not impossible that he became a hero to Pennsylvanians by way of London. That he had at least a modicum of popularity in Pennsylvania is evident from the fact that Christopher Sauer published a German translation of an English biography of the Prussian king in 1761.[89]

Likenesses of Frederick, probably in the form of engravings, must also have been available in Pennsylvania. The 1767 inventory of the bookbinder Abraham Myer of Lancaster includes, at a low evaluation, "a Picketr of the Kinge of Prusia—0 3 6."[90]

Shortly after the middle of the century an equestrian figure was cast into a stove plate at the Shearwell Furnace in the Oley Valley of Berks County (Fig. 98). No identification of the horseman is given on the plate, but since it and the pot of flowers next to it are posed beneath arches very much like those found on chests, it is easy to imagine the iron plate being a model for chest decorators.

With the coming of the War for Independence, the horse and rider also may have appeared on furniture as symbols of the spirit of rebellion. A chest now in the Smithsonian Institution is decorated with two horsemen who could be Continental Army soldiers (Fig. 102). After 1775 many pictures of George Washington on horseback were printed, and this new image replaces the old European one of the monarch or field marshal. Engraved "portraits" of Washington are found quite soon in the stock of European dealers, and some of these may have found their way back to the new United States. Neatly labeled, so that there is no question of his identity, Washington also appears in the work of at least one of the back-country Pennsylvania Fraktur writers (Fig. 99).

The motif of the rider also appears one time on a hand-drawn birth and baptismal certificate and several times on sgraffito plates. On the certificate we are told that he is hunting for the Crown of Righteousness (Fig. 100). On the plates he admits to a more profane pursuit— women (Fig. 101). Since overtly religious motifs are so rare on chests, it is the secular idea which is most likely behind the use of the man on horseback on most of the furniture. Only one time (Fig. 133) does the double equestrian figure—a man and a woman both riding the same horse—appear on Pennsylvania-German furniture. Since the motif is painted on a chest, it is quite possibly an allusion to the *Hochzeitszug*, or wedding procession. This event, the groom carrying his bride back from the wedding ceremony to the reception which followed, is depicted in German art as early as the fifteenth century (Fig. 134).

Although it is frequently seen on birth and baptismal certificates (Fig. 149), the *Nixe*, or mermaid, has been found on only one chest, that made for Anne Beer in 1790 (Figs. 147–149).[91] German folk tales are the clue to the use of the motif on both items related to birth and to the household (Fig. 148). In some areas of Germany the water creature was believed to dwell at the bottom of small bodies of water with herds of unborn babies. When the time for a birth drew near, the midwife would visit the spring, lake, or brook and the *Nixe* would deliver up a baby to her.[92] It is certainly probable that this belief persisted among some of the Pennsylvania Germans.[93] A reading of folk tales indicates an additional reason why the *Nixe*, as one of the genus *Wassergeist*, may have been used on an item of household furniture. Although often mean in nature, the creature could be cajoled into helping men with their household chores—all except the making of beds.[94]

If the chest was to be decorated with anything other than plain paint or texturing, the overall designs of the panels framing the designs —and sometimes the motifs—were plotted on the bare wood. Most of the surviving chests show evidence of scribing in the wood before the application of the ground coat. A very sharp instrument, such as a very pointed knife blade or a compass point, was used to scribe the lines. These lines usually show clearly through the paint, and were used to guide the hand of the decorator during the final brushwork. Some decorators followed the lines very carefully. Others wandered on either side of their guidelines as frequently as not. Some of the chest decorators—the unicorn painters of Berks County, for example—also had templates for the major elements of their designs (Figs. 84–91). The large tulip blossoms and the unicorns on a number of the Berks chests are so close in size and shape that it is apparent the same pattern was used in plotting the design on several chests. Unfortunately, none of the actual patterns used by any of the decorators of chests have been preserved. If some do survive, they have not yet been recognized as what they really are. They would probably have been cut from thin wood veneer or from thin sheet metal.

Several decorators of reasonable ability—Christian Selzer, for one —only scribed the outlines of the panels on their chests. The lines of the floral and other motifs were brushed in freehand or over pencil or chalk drawings which would have been obliterated in the act of painting.

Two or three of the chest decorators used carved blocks to transfer designs to the surfaces of their furniture. Carved probably from wood, the blocks were dipped into a thick paint or tinted varnish mixture and then pressed against the sides and fronts of the chests. One of the craftsmen used his blocks of men or horses and small floral or snowflake designs to imprint motifs in white and red in brilliant contrast to the dark blue or green of the background paint (Figs. 111, 112, and 207). Another, working some thirty years later, used floral blocks to imprint a wispy design in dark brown on the lighter brown of the undercoat (Fig. 168). The resulting effect achieved by the second decorator is very much like that of an old wallpaper.

The use of stencils is hardly ever observed on Pennsylvania-German chests of the eighteenth and early nineteenth centuries. One decorator who did use them, however, employed them to form only the crisp outlines of the astragal end panels on the fronts of his chests (Fig. 115). After the second decade of the nineteenth century, however, stenciling is frequently used in lieu of freehand painting. It is obviously used as a time-saving device and as such is one of the heralds of the decline of the traditional arts of rural Pennsylvania.

The abraded condition of the surfaces of most chests, and the fact that many of them have been given new surface coatings in this century, make it almost impossible to tell if they were varnished or shellacked just after painting. The application of a sealing and protecting finish—which would be more common on a piece made of hardwood—may have been the exception rather than the rule for painted pieces. The paint itself was probably considered the protective coating for the wood. The chest made for Ludwig Raub (Fig. 229), which is in a superlative state of preservation, shows, however, that varnish was indeed sometimes used over paint. The finish on this particular chest seems to have been applied quite early, possibly by the maker. It is a very thin coat of varnish that has yellowed with time and the inevitable accumulation of surface dirt. The finish has served its protective purpose admirably, and, underneath, the original red, white, and green of the painted decoration is still brilliant.

Since only a relatively small number of Pennsylvania-German chests are signed or initialed, disappointingly few can be attributed to the hands of specific craftsmen. In the course of this study only nine or ten men could be singled out as the makers of specific pieces with any degree of certainty. Peter Rohn (Figs. 81–82) was at work in Northampton County in the eighteenth century. The artist "JF" and possibly an associate were at work in Lancaster County just slightly later (Figs. 135–138, 225). At least five painters were working in or near Jonestown, Lebanon County, at the end of the eighteenth century and the beginning of the nineteenth (Figs. 105–110, 210–212) while Joel Palmer (Figs. 191–193, 250) and Christian Blauch (Fig. 194) were situated on the extreme fringes of the area of traditional Germanic influence. Both were working at about the middle of the nineteenth century or later.

When first recorded and published, Peter Rohn's name was misread from an inscription in a chest as "Peter Rahn."[95] Since the chest had been found in Bucks County, an unsuccessful search for information about him was made in that area. With the correct reading of his name, however, it became apparent that he probably worked near Easton in Northampton County.[96] Since this is not too far from the northern line of Bucks County the appearance of his work there is relatively easy to explain.

A sizeable group of chests bear an inscription that translates, "This chest belongs to me. . . ." At least two artists seem to have been involved in their decoration, but both have the same initials. The chest painted for Rael Hummer is signed "Jo" and "Fl," and those painted for Abraham Brubacher and Jacob Dres bear the initials "JF." All the chests in the group were made for families living in the Maytown, Manheim, Mt. Joy area of Lancaster County. One of the likeliest candidates as decorator of some of the chests is John Flory, a resident of Rapho Township. He is listed on the county tax lists as a joiner from 1789 to 1824.[97] Besides those mentioned above, there are also chests inscribed for Rahel Friedrich (1791),[98] Daniel Rickert (1791), Pedras Schneider (1791), Susana Badrof (1792),[99] [Se]bastian Keller (1793), Veronica Ober˙(1794),[100] and Maria Witmer (1800).

If there was ever a "school" of Pennsylvania-German chest decoration, it was seated in Jonestown, Dauphin (now Lebanon) County, between the early 1770's and the end of the second decade of the nineteenth century. During those years, four (or possibly five) decorators worked in or near the town. What is even more extraordinary is that all of them signed almost every piece of their work and dated it as well.

How convenient it would be for researchers if this artistic vanity had been prevalent everywhere in southeastern Pennsylvania.

Four of the five decorators were from two families. Christian Selzer (February 16, 1749–February 3, 1831) and John Selzer (August 9, 1774–February 1, 1845) were father and son. John Rank (April 15, 1763–May 4, 1828) and Peter Rank (November 3, 1765–June 26, 1851) were brothers. John Selzer—compounding the relationships—was married to a Sarah Rank.

Nothing is known of the fifth decorator except his name. Inscribed on the one chest found from his hand, it appears to be "Michel Stoot" or "Michel Stout."[101] Dated 1788, the panels of the chest are inspired by the work of the elder Selzer, so it is presumed the copyist worked nearby.

We do not know if Christian Selzer was a woodworker who made his own furniture. It is likely. That his son John was a craftsman in wood we know from his brother Christian Jr.'s will written in 1814. John is referred to as "of Bethel Township" and as a "House Carpenter."[102] The inventory of John's estate, taken on February 6, 1845, includes:

a lot of Boards	1.50
Plaining bench & carpenter tools	4.50
?̲ chisel	.25
Woodsaw	.25
6 axes	1.87½[103]

There is also no documentation to indicate that John Rank did any cabinetwork, but we do know from the physical evidence that he certainly painted more than a few. In his will, signed in March of 1828, he calls himself "Innkeeper."[104] The inn which he bequeathed to his son John he described as "Situate in Jone's Town on the North west corner of Market and Broad Street." The inventory of his estate gives no evidence of any career in woodworking.

Only in the case of John Peter Rank do we have evidence to prove that he made chests as well as painted them. In the rare book collection of the Winterthur Museum library is a manuscript account book that he used at least from March 5, 1794 to December, 1814.[105] On the inside of one cover is the inscription, "Peter Rank his Book." The inside of the other cover bears the name of Daniel Arnd, but from internal evidence it is clear that the book was used mainly by Rank. Included in it are nicely detailed drawings of a chest of drawers and a tall clock in the style sometimes attributed to the Bachmans of Lancaster County. Also in it are a number of entries that give evidence of the range of Rank's woodworking and the prices that he charged. That Rank's first language was not English is evident.

Early in the account book Rank noted that "Richert Stepns is intetet to me for one Cofing The Sum of 0/15/0." Shortly after that Rank must have laid a floor for a customer, since he wrote: "Mikkele Simmerman is intetet for liing is flour and et comes to 0/11/3." On July 16, 1796, Rank noted, "Andey Wilson is intetet to mie for duing the jinner work of his House the Sum of £ 55: 0: 0 pounds Peter Rank." The signature is in the same hand as the preceding notation, leaving no doubt that the book is indeed that of Peter Rank.

What may be a reference to an accumulation of dowry furniture is noted the following year when Rank wrote: "Marge 29 1797 and I Mite fore valentine Shoufler to one Christ at £ 1: 13: 9 [;] to one Diple [table] and et comes to 1: 10: 0 [;] to one pit Stodt [bedstead] and et comes to 1: 5: 0 [;] to one thot traft [dough trough] and et comes to 0: 10:" That same year a relative began to assist in either the shop or the inn, for Rank wrote, "Deniel Ranck pegan to vork in Julius 24 Day 1797."

On January 27, 1800, "Jacop Gremer began to vork as a *prindis*." Later in the same year Philip Krips was charged with £2.5.0. for "one Chist with drawers," and on "March 18the 1814" John Groh purchased two "Chist with drawers" for £7.10.0.

In Rank's accountbook there are only two mentions of paint in connection with chests. After making and painting a bedstead for George Mink, Rank wrote: "to one gist and one lock and pinding [painting] and et comes to 0 6 6." The second entry concerning the painting of a chest reads, "Make lena [Magdalena] Walporn pinting one chist 0 5 0." Both entries were made in 1807.

Inserted in the account book is a small piece of paper—seemingly in Peter Rank's handwriting—labeled, "The Gentlemens Bill." Oats, Hay, "Soper," Lodging and "Brickfist" are listed for a total of £0.12.3.

This and a number of entries dealing with food and drink indicate clearly that Peter was involved with his brother John in the management of the family business, Jonestown's White Horse Tavern, or ran another.[106]

Near the outer limits of Pennsylvania chest decoration—both geographically and chronologically—is the work of Joel Palmer. He was born in 1812 and was living in Belfast Township, Fulton County, when he died in 1884. While he is the only Anglo-American craftsman of decorated chests that we know by name, an American of English background decorating furniture in the manner associated only with the Germans of Pennsylvania is not as unusual as it may seem. After February, 1847, Palmer painted several chests in commemoration of the Battle of Buena Vista. A half-dozen of his chests have been found in the area between Needmore, Pennsylvania, and Hancock, Maryland.[107]

Dated and signed examples of decorated furniture are occasionally found bearing the name of Christian Blauch. Almost nothing is known of him, except that he was probably working in Conemaugh Township, Cambria County or in Somerset County.[108]

Outside Pennsylvania

Until well into the nineteenth century Pennsylvania remained the most fertile area for the practice of the Germanic decorative arts in America, although other sections of the country with sizeable German populations also produced an appreciable amount of applied decoration in the Old-World tradition. The Germans of Maryland, Ohio, Virginia, and North Carolina all patronized craftsmen whose work might be mistaken for that of their countrymen in Pennsylvania.

The Mason-Dixon line is a boundary only on paper and in legal proceedings; thus the culture of German Pennsylvania easily spilled over into northern Maryland. That portion of the state which lies west of an imaginary line drawn between York, Pennsylvania, and Baltimore, Maryland, was and is the home of thousands of Americans descended from eighteenth-century German immigrants. Fraktur in both German and English is encountered in the western counties of Maryland, and decorated chests are not unknown from the same area. One such chest (Fig. 41), which is said to have been found near Frederick, is in the rare sgraffito style. Interestingly enough, when this same style of decoration has been found in Pennsylvania it has been in southern York County, near the northern border of Maryland. It is certainly not impossible that more than one piece of painted furniture thought to have been made in Pennsylvania was actually created across the line in a German community in Maryland.

Numbers of Pennsylvania Germans joined the migration into the western territories in the late eighteenth and early nineteenth centuries. Many settled in the eastern and southern parts of what became the state of Ohio in 1803. Since most undoubtedly brought with them at least some household goods, it is not surprising that numbers of Pennsylvania-German-style decorated chests have been reported found in Ohio. Sometimes it is not at all easy to ascertain whether the particular piece was brought from Pennsylvania or was made in Ohio. In 1817, a newly arrived group of religious separatists from Württemburg founded a community at Zoar, Ohio, and added a fresh stream of influence to the decorative arts tradition from Pennsylvania. Even so, painted furniture of a distinctly German character is much rarer in Ohio than it is further east.

Virginia's first organized group of German immigrants arrived in the Spring of 1714.[109] More followed, coming directly from Europe or south from Pennsylvania and Maryland. Heavily German areas developed in the Shenandoah Valley, and in them, as one might expect, the traditional decorative arts were practiced. Research in Shenandoah County and also in Wythe County in southwestern Virginia has turned up considerable numbers of painted and inlaid pieces of furniture. Enough has been discovered in the latter area to enable researchers to attribute a group of items, both chests and clock cases, to one Johannes Spitler. Born in Wythe County in 1774, Spitler moved to Ohio between 1805 and 1809. His furniture, painted in a most individualistic manner, is often initialed and numbered (Fig. 44).[110]

At least one other decorator working in Wythe County appears to have used a chest by one of the Jonestown, Pennsylvania, painters as his model (Fig. 45). The Virginia copy is complete even to a scratched inscription in one of the painted vases (Fig. 46). Three chests are known from the hand of this painter. All are dated 1829, and all have locks initialed "J.D."

At least one of the seldom-seen walnut chests with non-wood inlay was also made in Virginia, and at a relatively late date. Made by Godfrey Wilkin of Hardy County (now in West Virginia) for a relative, the chest is inlaid with a witty and meandering inscription. On either end are inlaid the words, "WEL DON." The inlay is called "putty" in the records of the institution which owns it, but as yet no laboratory tests have been done to determine the composition of the material. The construction of the chest is quite unorthodox in that the paneled front is hinged at the bottom and drops down to reveal storage drawers. The chest is certainly not a classic German furniture form.

At an early date North Carolina also became home for large numbers of Germans. One would expect to find numerous decorated chests in this area, but this is not the case. Only a few have been identified as being of North Carolina origin. Many of the immigrants who settled there were Moravian, members of the *Unitas Fratrum,* and so the situation which holds for this group in Pennsylvania applies also in North Carolina. For whatever the reason, there is no Moravian Fraktur of any great consequence, nor is there any Moravian painted furniture from the American settements. This is certainly all the more surprising since, as observed earlier, there were workshops for the production of elaborate painted furniture in the Moravian headquarters town of Herrnhut in Saxony.

Those chests that have been found in North Carolina may or may not resemble chests known to be from Pennsylvania. One chest (Fig. 47) was even twice sold as a Pennsylvania chest though both antique dealers involved knew that it had been found in North Carolina. The vividly scrolled bracket base—uncharacteristic for Pennsylvania chests—and the use of southern wood in its construction, however, do justify it being considered a chest made in the southern state. Another pine chest-on-frame from North Carolina has typical "Pennsylvania" six-pointed stars painted on it. They almost seem to be an afterthought and are rather crude decoration on a fairly sophisticated piece of furniture. The form of chest on a frame has never been found decorated with paint in Pennsylvania.

Although the brightly decorated chest was almost completely out of fashion with Germans in America when the second wave of immigrants arrived in the second quarter of the nineteenth century, some of them did indeed have chests made for themselves. Such is the case with the chest made either in Ohio or Indiana for Philip Hirschy. Born in Canton Neuenburg, Switzerland, he came to the United States in 1835. Settling first in Ohio, he moved to Indiana about the time the chest was made for him (Fig. 49).[111] The chest reflects nothing of the colorful and sprightly country decoration still being done in Switzerland at the time. It is a chaste piece of decoration—at home with American "country Empire" furniture—and is painted in imitation of the veneer so popular here toward mid-century.

In rural Pennsylvania, as in other areas of the United States and Canada with large German populations, the traditional decorative arts brought by the original immigrants began to die out in the second and third decades of the nineteenth century. What had been preserved by isolation was now eroded by intercourse with the urban centers. Decorated furniture, along with building crafts the most visible of the Old-World traditions, was among the first to suffer from the inroads of urban taste and fashion. The more intimate of the crafts, Fraktur-writing and needlework, would linger on in many are as until late in the century, but painted furniture, except for the decorated plank seat chair, became more and more ordinary and uninteresting. The chest and wardrobe are the most elaborately decorated of the furnishings in the rural Pennsylvania household from about 1760 to 1825. Those made after that time are somber reflections of their predecessors. Hearts and flowers and birds were replaced with two-toned graining or with mahogany veneers. Except for the unexpected exuberance of a craftsman such as Joel Palmer outside the mainstream of the Pennsylvania-German community, the unabashed gaudiness of the early furniture was replaced with a sober tonality that reflected much of the manners and morals of nineteenth-century America (Figs. 191–193).

The chest form did remain useful into the twentieth century in many a household. Many of the old pieces, however, were overpainted in one color as the elaborate decoration dear to an earlier generation was considered old-fashioned or a cause of embarrassment in front of city cousins. As stylish new factory-made furniture was acquired, many of the old chests were relegated to the attic, cellar, or even to barns and chicken houses. Many were worn or weathered beyond restoration by being used as woodboxes and feed bins. About fifty years ago, however, the Pennsylvania-German decorative arts were "discovered" by American collectors and museum curators. There was a wholesale reevaluation of our country arts and crafts. Noteworthy chests were ferreted out at country auctions and antique shops. Families which had decorated chests began to bring them out to be admired as valued heirlooms or as eminently saleable items. A history of the development of interest in Pennsylvania-German things in our time would be as interesting as the stories of the objects themselves. Since the first painted chests went into the collection of major American museums their value as exemplary examples of American furniture has risen considerably. There can be no question but that they are one of the great glories of the decorative arts in rural America.

Notes to the Text

1. The Pennsylvania-German word *Shonk* is a dialectical variant of the High German *Schrank*. Either is a word more appropriate for this piece of furniture than the frequently encountered Holland-Dutch word *Kas*.

2. Leopold Schmidt, *Bauernmöbel aus Süddeutschland, Österreich und der Schweiz* (Vienna: Forum Verlag, 1967), p. 42.

3. Gislind M. Ritz, *The Art of Painted Furniture* (New York: Van Nostrand Reinhold Co., 1971), pp. 11–12. Otto Bramm, "Truhentypen," *Volkswerk, Jahrbuch des Staat-Museums für Deutsche Volkskunde* (Jena: Eugen Diederichs Verlag, 1941), map between pp. 172–73.

4. Albert Walzer,"Baden-württembergische Bauernmöbel, Teil II," *Der Museumsfreund* 10/11 (1969): 17, 20.

5. Schmidt, p. 31.

6. Ibid, p. 42.

7. Ritz, pp. 11–12.

8. Bramm, pp. 158–61; Ritz, p. 11.

9. Bramm, pp. 161–64.

10. Ritz, pp. 7–12.

11. *Minutes of the Provincial Council of Pennsylvania*, vol. 3 (Philadelphia, 1852), pp. 28–29.

12. Ibid., pp. 282–83.

13. Ralph Beaver Strassburger and William John Hinke, *Pennsylvania German Pioneers* (Norristown, Pa.: Pennsylvania German Society, 1934), p. xxxi.

14. Otto Langguth and Don Yoder, "Pennsylvania German Pioneers from the County of Wertheim," *The Pennsylvania German Folklore Society* 12 (1947): 187–88, 225–26.

15. Strassburger and Hinke, p. 21.

16. *Pennsylvanische Berichte*, November 16, 1749, p. 3, col. 1, quoted in *Proceedings of the Pennsylvania German Society* 10 (1900): 206.

17. Robert Hunter Morris (c. 1700–1764) received the governorship of Pennsylvania from John and Thomas Penn in 1754. He quarreled with the Assembly from the start of his term in office and resigned in 1756.

18. Christopher Sauer (1693–1758) is the eldest of three family members with the same name.

19. Frank Reid Diffenderffer, "The German Immigration into Pennsylvania through the Port of Philadelphia from 1700 to 1775," *Proceedings of the Pennsylvania German Society* 10 (1900): 241.

20. This business was, of course, the defense of the Province. England and France went to war in the spring of 1754 and at the time Sauer's letter was written the enemy was harassing the Pennsylvania frontier. General Edward Braddock's defeat was only two months away.

21. It would be a long time before any action were taken to redress the grievances of the immigrants. Not until the founding of the German Society of Pennsylvania on Chistmas Day, 1764, was there an organization of Germans strong enough to force political action in the Province. On May 18, 1765, Governor John Penn finally signed a law protecting immigrants both while at sea and after arriving in Pennsylvania.

22. This indeed was the case. The Pennsylvania-German farmer fought side-by-side with his English-speaking neighbors during the entire war.

23. Just a year earlier a scheme had been initiated for organizing free schools for the German youths of Pennsylvania. Sauer was one of the most outspoken of those who saw the scheme as a conspiracy to Anglicize rather than educate.

24. Diffenderffer, pp. 249–54.

25. Monroe H. Fabian, "An Immigrant's Inventory," *Pennsylvania Folklife* 15 (Summer, 1976): 47–48.

26. Could it be found, a chest that was made for one Maria Katharina Lefever would be of great interest, since it was dated 1755. Her husband Daniel, in a deed of settlement, described it as, "one flowered popular [sic] chest marked as before and the date 1755 thereon." Pewter listed earlier had been described as marked "MKLF" and evidently the chest was also so

initialed—indicating that it had been acquired after the wedding. [Lancaster County Court House, Deed Book M, 1:247–48.]

27. I am indebted to Dr. Heidi Müller for her comments and for introducing me to Friederich Sieber's very important small book about the Herrnhut furniture, *Bunte Möbel der Oberlausitz* ([East] Berlin: Akademie-Verlag, 1955).

28. Thomas Chippendale, *The Gentleman and Cabinet-Maker's Director*, revised and enlarged third edition (London, 1762), p. 126. The engraving had actually been prepared in 1753.

29. Maurice Tomlin, *English Furniture, an Illustrated Handbook* (London: Faber and Faber, 1972), pp. 36, 37, 49, 57, 64, 74.

30. For discussions of various aspects of the problem, see John D. Morse, ed., *Winterthur Conference Report 1969: Country Cabinetwork and Simple City Furniture* (Charlottesville: The University Press of Virginia, 1970).

31. Bryden B. Hyde, *Bermuda's Antique Furniture and Silver* (Hamilton: Bermuda National Trust, 1971), pp. 106–31.

32. Ritz, p. 11.

33. Berks County Court House, Will A 360, 1797.

34. Lebanon County Court House, Will of John George Wolfesbarger, filed January 2, 1817.

35. Raymond E. Hollenbach, " 'S Pennsylvaanisch Deitsch Eck," *Allentown Morning Call*, December 5, 1964.

36. Ibid.

37. Raymond E. Hollenbach and Alan G. Keyser, eds., *The Account Book of the Clemens Family* (Breinigsville, Pa.: The Pennsylvania German Society, 1975).

38. Gerhart Clemens's wife was Anneli Reif, stepdaughter of Hans Stauffer, whom he married in Europe in 1702. Stauffer, a Mennonite from Zurich who was living in Alsace, wrote in his account book, "I gave Anel two guldens for the chest, 1703, August." It would seem that this chest was not acquired until after the wedding. In 1709 Hans Stauffer, his family, and that of another daughter, also journeyed to America. [William T. Stauffer, "Hans Stauffer's Account Books," *Publications of the Genealogical Society of Pennsylvania* 10 (March, 1929): 296–302.]

39. Hollenbach and Keyser, p. 38.

40. Ibid., pp. 38–67.

41. Ibid., pp. 90–117.

42. Theodore W. Jentsch, "Old Order Mennonite Family Life in the East Penn Valley," *Pennsylvania Folklife* 24 (Autumn, 1974): 18–27.

43. "Die Historie, wie man sie aus Elisabeth Joderin zu Oly, ihrem eigenen Munde geschrieben Anno 1743 . . . ," *Verschiedene alte und neuere Geschichten von Erscheinungen der Geister.* . . . , published and probably compiled by Christopher Sauer (Germantown, 1755), pp. 33–38. First published in 1744, the book appeared in a number of editions. I have used a Library of Congress microfilm of the 1755 edition in the American Antiquarian Society.

44. Most of the inventory citations in the foregoing section were provided from the research files of Mrs. Ellen Gehret and Alan G. Keyser. I am indebted to them for their cooperation.

45. A case in point is Ephrahim Benedikt Garbel, who is called "master cabinetmaker" in papers filed when he was obtaining permission to emigrate to America in April of 1753. He arrived at Philadelphia aboard the *Neptune* in September of that year and was later resident in Lancaster. [Langguth and Yoder, p. 218.]

46. *Gottlieb Mittelberger's Journey to Pennsylvania in the Year 1750 and Return to Germany in 1754. . .* , Carl Theo. Eben, tr. (Philadelphia: John Joseph McVey, 1898), p. 56.

47. Abraham Overholt's Account Book, manuscript owned by Robert C. Bucher, translated by Alan G. Keyser.

48. Henry Chapman Mercer, *Ancient Carpenters' Tools* (New York: Horizon Press, 1975), p. xi.

49. *Encyclopedia Britannica*, 14th ed., s.v. "tulip tree" and "poplar."

50. Ibid., s.v. "walnut."

51. Walzer, p. 15.

52. Patrick M'Roberts, "Tour through the North Provinces of America," Carl Bridenbaugh, ed., *The Pennsylvania Magazine of History and Biography* 59 (1935): 134–80.

53. Carl Bridenbaugh, *The Colonial Craftsman* (New York: New York University Press, 1950), p. 61.

54. Arthur Cecil Bining, *Pennsylvania Iron Manufacture in the Eighteenth Century* (Harrisburg: Pennsylvania Historical and Museum Commission, 1973), p. 165.

55. Arthur Cecil Bining, *British Regulation of the Colonial Iron Industry* (Philadelphia: University of Pennsylvania Press, 1933) p. 132 and Appendix C.

56. *Pennsylvanische Berichte*, August 16, 1755, p. 3, col. 2.

57. Henry J. Kauffman, *Early American Hardware, Cast and Wrought* (Rutland, Vt.: Charles E. Tuttle Co., 1966), p. 107.

58. Margaret Berwind Schiffer, *Furniture and Its Makers of Chester County, Pennsylvania* (Philadelphia: University of Pennsylvania Press, 1966), p. 275.

59. *Pennsylvania Gazette*, August 3, 1749.

60. Ibid., April 28, 1727.

61. Ibid., April 11, 1749.

62. For a complete coverage of this episode in American commercial history, see Arthur M. Schlesinger, *The Colonial Merchants and the American Revolution, 1763–1776* (New York: Atheneum Publishers, 1968).

63. Charles F. Hummel, "Samuel Rowland Fisher's Catalogue of English Hardware," *Winterthur Portfolio* 1 (1964): 188–97.

64. F. Lewis Hinckley, *Directory of Historic Cabinet Woods* (New York: Crown Publishers, 1960), p. 20.

65. Charles F. Montgomery, *American Furniture, The Federal Period* (New York: The Viking Press, 1966), p. 33.

66. Frances Lichten, "A Masterpiece of Pennsylvania-German Furniture," *Antiques* 77 (February, 1960): 176–78.

67. Monroe H. Fabian, "Sulfur Inlay in Pennsylvania-German Furniture," *Pennsylvania Folklife* 27 (Autumn, 1977): 2–9.

68. Dean A. Fales, Jr., *American Painted Furniture, 1660–1880* (New York: E. P. Dutton and Co., 1972), p. 10.

69. For a comprehensive discussion see Benjamin L. Miller, *The*

Mineral Pigments of Pennsylvania (Harrisburg: Topographic and Geologic Survey of Pennsylvania, 1911).

70. Theodore Zuk Penn, "Decorative and Protective Finishes, 1750–1850: Materials, Process, and Craft," (M.A. diss., University of Delaware, 1966). Most of the notes on pigments in this section of the book are abstracted from this valuable study.

71. *Pennsylvania Gazette*, March 26, 1741, p. 6, col. 1.

72. Ibid., June 25, 1747, p. 3, col. 3.

73. Rosamund D. Harley, *Artists' Pigments, c. 1600–1835* (London: Butterworth & Co., 1970), p. 116.

74. Ibid., p. 125.

75. Ibid., p. 85.

76. Ibid., p. 91–92.

77. *Pennsylvania Packet*, November 6, 1789.

78. Harley, p. 54.

79. Ibid., pp. 76–77.

80. Ibid., p. 93.

81. Ibid., p. 95.

82. Ritz, pp. 141–44.

83. Johann Krauss, *Oeconomisches Haus-und Kunst-Buch . . .*, (Allentown, Pa.: Heinrich Ebner, 1819), pp. 436–38.

84. Richard M. Candee, "The Rediscovery of Milk-based House Paints and the Myth of 'Brickdust and Buttermilk' Paints," *Old-Time New England* 58 (Fall, 1967): 79–81.

85. Ritz, p. 12.

86. Rüdiger Robert Beer, *Einhorn, Fablewelt und Wirklichkeit* (Munich: Verlag Georg W. Callwey, 1972).

87. In the German sagas, the unicorn is said to have charged wildly in a struggle with a lion and got his horn stuck in a tree. This tale may explain the positioning of the unicorn against a tree on the chests. It may also be the reason why it is often paired with a lion. [*Handwörterbuch des deutscher Aberglaubens* (Berlin: Walter de Gruyter & Co., 1938–1941), abt. 1, vol. 9, cols. 127–91.]

88. James Evelyn Pilcher, *The Seal and Arms of Pennsylvania* (Harrisburg: The State of Pennsylvania, 1902), pp. 12–13.

89. Christopher Sauer, tr., *Das Leben und Heroische Thaten Des Königs von Preussen Friederichs des III. . . . Zuerst in Englischer Sprache heraus gegeben durch W. H. Dilworth 1758 und nun ins Deutsche übersetzt und vermehrt.*

90. Lancaster County Register of Wills, inventory of the estate of Abraham Myer, filed April 15, 1767.

91. The 1810 census lists members of the Beer family in what are now Allen and Lehigh Townships, Lehigh County, and in Towamensing Township, Carbon County. The chest was found in that general area and may have been made there.

92. *Handwörterbuch des deutschen Aberglaubens*, s.v., "Wassergeister."

93. In May, 1976, Dr. Philip Hershey of York County informed the author that when he was a child, about 1910, his father was a physician in Wrightstown. Whenever his father left during the night to deliver a baby, he would tell his son that he was going down to Pier 8 on the Susquehanna to fish a baby out of the water for someone. Little Philip fretted during winter months wondering how the babies in the water would be protected from the ice that frequently covered the river in those days. At the time, there were ferry boats on the river, and whenever Philip was on one that passed near Pier 8 he would lean over the rail hoping to see the babies under the water. Although there is no mention of a water-creature in the story, it does seem that the old German folk tale, at least in part, was remembered in Pennsylvania into the present century.

94. *Handwörterbuch des deutschen Aberglaubens*, s.v., "Wassergeister."

95. John Cummings, "Painted Chests from Bucks County," *Pennsylvania Folklife* 9 (Summer, 1958): 20–23.

96. A Peter Rohn, who was born in 1761 or 1762, was confirmed in Dryland Church, Nazareth Township, Northampton County, November 4, 1781. He was married before February 25, 1787, on which date he stood with his wife as a baptismal sponsor in the same church. He died August 21, 1834, "on the Dryland in the 72nd year of his age." [Church book, Dryland Reformed Church; *Easton Sentinel*, August 29, 1834.]

97. The church book of the Zion Lutheran Church in Manheim contains a transcript of a contract between the church council and the carpenters John Flory and Andrew Shell for pews for the church. The contract is dated August 26, 1780. The carpenter is probably the John Flory who was born May 3, 1754, the son of Johannes Flory and Anna Danker Flory. This is also most likely the Johannes Flory, Jr., listed with married communicants at Manheim on May 23, 1779. On April 24, 1781, a John Flory and Susanna are listed as the sponsors for Susanna Margretha Bender, child of Adam and Barbara Bender. On April 8, 1794, a Johannes Flory (probably a different man) married Anna Stauffer in Trinity Lutheran Church, Lancaster. It is not impossible that the county tax lists carry the names of more than one person named John Flory, perhaps father and son or uncle and nephew, working at the same trade in the same area. [Church book, Zion Lutheran Church, Manheim; Church book, Trinity Lutheran Church, Lancaster; Lancaster County Tax Assessments.]

98. This is probably the Rael Frederick who was married to Michael Schetterle in Trinity Lutheran Church, Lancaster, March 4, 1800. [Church book, Trinity Lutheran Church, Lancaster.]

99. This is probably the Susanna Barbara Battruff who was born September 28, 1772 and baptized October 25, 1772 in Zion Lutheran Church, Manheim. Her parents were Andreas Battruff and his wife Christina Sophia. The sponsors were Susanna Baumann and Hartman Morris. [Church book, Zion Lutheran Church, Manheim.]

100. This is most likely the Veronica Ober born January 19, 1784, a daughter of Henrich and Veronica Ober. Her Fraktur birth certificate (no baptism is mentioned since she was Mennonite), written by the schoolmaster J. F. S. Gebhard and dated March 29, 1790, is still in the possession of descendants.

101. The 1790 census lists the name "Stout" in Dauphin County and the name "Stroot" over the line in Bethel Township, Berks County.

102. Register of Wills, Lebanon County, S-7.

103. Ibid., Inventory S-265.

104. Ibid., R-18.

105. Manuscript Account Book, shelf no. 67 x 23, Winterthur Museum Library.

106. Esther S. Fraser, "Pennsylvania German Dower Chests," *Antiques* 11 (February, 1927): 123.

107. Register of Wills, Fulton County; Conversations with Mary Bridges Vann and Charles Henry; Gray Boone, notes concerning Joel Palmer in the column "Purely Personal," *Antique Monthly* (July, 1971): 1c.

108. He may be the Christian Blauch who died in Conemaugh Boro in 1869. A Christian Blough was born in Somerset County in 1822 and was still living there in 1906. [Register of Wills, Cambria County Court House; E. Howard Blackburn and W. H. Welfley, *History of Bedford and Somerset Counties, Pennsylvania*, vol. 2 (New York: Lewis Publishing Co., 1906), p. 533.

109. Klaus Wust, *The Virginia Germans* (Charlottesville: University of Virginia Press, 1969), p. 20.

110. Donald Walters, "Johannes Spitler, Shenandoah County, Furniture Decorator," *Antiques* 108 (October, 1975): 730–35.

111. Obituary of Philip Hirschy, *The Berne* (Indiana) *Witness*, October 19, 1899, courtesy of his descendant who owns the chest.

1. Arcaded chest with elaborate inlay and ironwork, from the southern Tirol, late 16th or early 17th century.
H. 41⅜ L. 78¾ D. 33½*

Tiroler Volkskunst-Museum, Innsbruck. Photo: Gratl.

2. Chest of carved oak highlighted with color, from Hallig Hooge, Schleswig-Holstein, 1751.
H. 20⅞ L. 40½ D. 18⅛
Germanisches Nationalmuseum, Nürnberg.

* All measurements are in inches.

3. *Frontalstollentruhe* of carved oak, from Borstel, Kreis Pinneberg, 1694.
H. 37¾ L. 55¾ D. 24½
Altonaer Museum, Hamburg.

4. Small *Seitstollentruhe* of painted softwood, Swiss, 1732.
H. 12¾ L. 20⅞ D. 7⅞
Schweizerisches Landesmuseum, Zurich.

The inscription translates as "This little chest belongs to me: Fellix Gietzendanner."

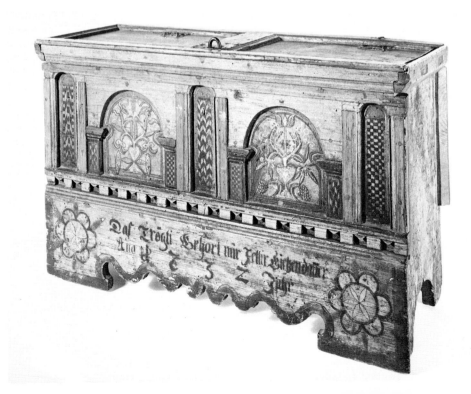

5. Arcaded *Kastentruhe* of painted softwood set on runners, probably made near Kassel, 1758.
   H. 24¾ L. 51¼ D. 25½
   Staatliche Kunstammlungen, Kassel.

   The two part inscription might be translated: "When two are in love everything is for the best."

6. *Kastentruhe* of painted softwood set on turned feet, Württemberg, 1781.
   H. 23½ L. 50⅞ D. 24¾
   Württembergisches Landesmuseum, Stuttgart.

7. *Kastentruhe* of painted softwood set on a *Sockel*, Swiss, 1782.
   H. 28¾ L. 50 D. 19¼
   Historisches Museum, Bern.

   Such a hunting scene is known on at least one chest painted in Pennsylvania (*See* Fig. 188). This chest was actually made in 1735 and overpainted in 1782.

8. *Kastentruhe* of painted softwood set on runners, Alsace, 1849.
   H. 24½ L. 56 D. 21½
   Musée Alsacien, Strasburg.

   Aside from the raised end pieces on the lid, this chest could easily pass for a Pennsylvania chest of fifty or sixty years earlier.

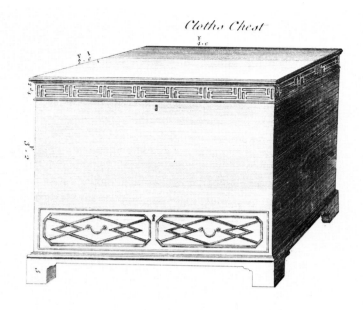

Cloths Chest

9. A chest over one drawer made to look like two.
A "Cloths Chest" in Thomas Chippendale's pattern book
published in London, 1762.
Henry Francis du Pont Winterthur Museum Libraries.

10. Chest over drawers, English, 18th century.
H. 29 L. 49¼ D. 22¼
Victoria and Albert Museum. Photo: Crown Copyright.

11. Chest over drawer, cedar, Bermuda, 18th century.
    H. 28 L. 49 D. 20
    Rupert Gentle. Photo: Studio Wreford.

12. Chest over drawers, Berks County, c. 1800, with printed broadside
    hand decorated by Friederich Speyer inside lid.
    Winterthur Museum.

3. Chest over drawers with stepped construction, oak with inlay of various woods, English, 18th century.
H. 36 L. 58 D. 22
Rupert Gentle. Photo: Studio Wreford.

14. Pennsylvania-German chest over drawers with stepped construction, painted softwood, late 18th century.
H. 30 L. 50 D. 24
Mr. and Mrs. E. Clifford Durell, Jr. Photo: Charles Maddox.

15. Swiss cradle and a chest with a tray-top lid. The chest is dated 1715 and is from the Sensebezirk near Freiburg.
Privately owned. Photo: Benedikt Rast.

16 (*above left*). Hinge from a chest dated 1764.

17 (*above right*). Hinge from a chest c. 1795.

18 (*left*). Hinge from a chest dated 1775.
Photo: Photo Optik.

89

19. Hinge from a chest dated 1773.
   Photo: Froelich Studio.

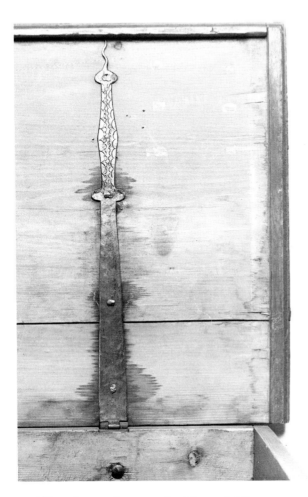

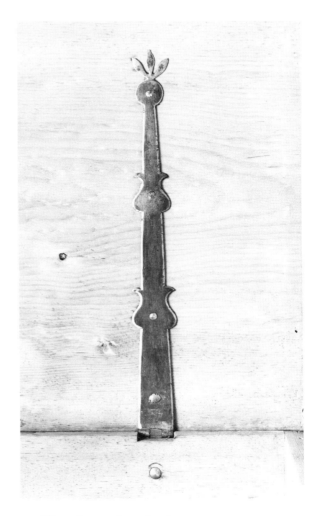

20. Hinge from a chest c. 1780. Photo: Cal Pane.

21. Hinge from a chest dated 1792.

22. Hinge from a chest c. 1810.
    Photo: Geoffrey Clements.

23. Hinge from a chest c. 1820.
    Photo: Photo Optik.

24. Back of a chest dated 1764, showing lower halves of the hinges.

25. Hinge attached to inside of lid and inside of back on a chest dated 1785.
Photo: James L. Dillon & Co.

26. Carrying handle on a chest dated 1791.
    Photo: Geoffrey Clements.

27. Carrying handle on a chest dated 1775.
    Photo: Geoffrey Clements.

28. Engraved crab lock on a chest dated 1764.

29. Box lock on a chest from the 1780's.
    Photo: Photo Optik.

30. Working side of a drawer lock removed from a chest dated 1772.
    Photo: Eugene Mantie.

31. Keyhole plate on a chest dated 1764.

32. Key to the same chest.

33 (*above*) and 34 (*below*). Details of a pair of hinges initialed "HS"
and dated 1792.
Privately owned. Photo: Photo Optik.

The hinges were removed from a chest said to have been found in
Lancaster County.

35. Lock stamped "IOSEPH STVMB" on a chest dated 1757.
Photo: Winterthur Museum Libraries. (*See* Fig. 52.)

36. Lock stamped "W. CLEWELL" on a chest c. 1820. (*See also* Fig. 181.)
Photo: Photo Optik.

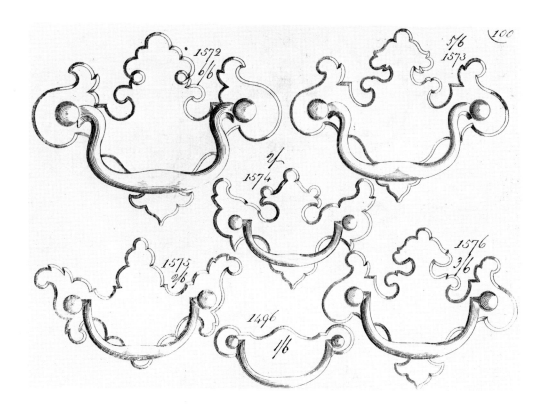

37 (*above*) and 38 (*below*). Two of the engraved plates illustrating brass
drawer pulls in the Samuel Rowland Fisher hardware catalogue. The
prices have been written in near each item.
Winterthur Museum Libraries.

39. Component parts of a brass drawer pull from a chest dated 1772.
    Photo: Eugene Mantie.

40. Pressed brass drawer pull on a chest c. 1830.
    Photo: Photo Optik.

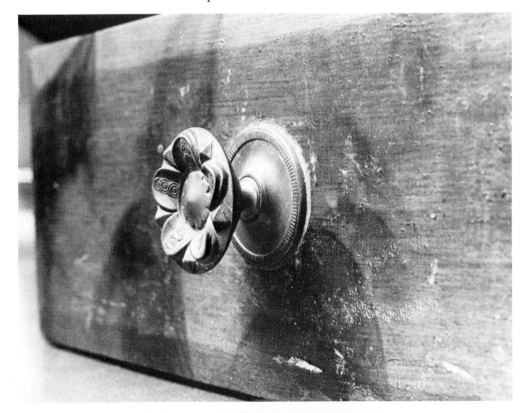

41. Chest found near Frederick, Maryland.
    Inscribed: J T/ADAM NEFF 1791
    H. 25¾ L. 49 D. 22⅜
    Museum of Early Southern Decorative Arts.

    The design is scratched through a thin coat of green paint to reveal
    the undercoat of orange.

42. Chest over drawers found in northern Ohio.
    H. 26½ L. 48½ D. 21½
    Ohio Historical Society.

43. Chest found in Ohio.
    H. 24⅜ L. 46 D. 20
    Ohio Historical Society.

44. Chest attributed to Johannes Spitler.
    Inscribed: x jSP x/1798/NO:48
    H. 24 L. 48⅞ D. 22
    Harvey L. Brumback. Photo: Abby Aldrich Rockefeller
    Folk Art Center.

46. Detail of the scratched inscription (*below*).
    Photo: Abby Aldrich Rockefeller Folk Art Center

45. Chest found in Virginia.
    Inscribed: [in left hand vase] 1829/Jahr
    H. 27¼ L. 50½ D. 22
    Richard and Mary Rhyne. Photo: Abby Aldrich Rockefeller Folk Art
    Center.

47. Chest found in North Carolina.
    Inscribed: B A T/A 13 D/1793
    H. 27 L. 49 D. 22
    Privately owned. Photo: Helga Photo Studio.

48. Chest on frame found in North Carolina.
H. 27¾ L. 48½ D. 19
Tryon Palace Restoration, New Bern, N.C.

49. Chest made in Ohio or Indiana.
Inscribed: P H/1846
H. 25 L. 52½ D. 21
Mrs. Richard Hirschy. Photo: Stedman Studio.

The arcs at the corners are in paint, but the name and date have been
stenciled in metallic powder or paint.

50. Chest, painted softwood.
    Inscribed: Anno 1729
    H. 17¾ L. 45½ D. 23½
    Schwenkfelder Museum. Photo: Camerique.

The earliest chests which have any history of use in Pennsylvania are
three that were brought by the Schwenkfelders in 1734. All three
chests were in the possession of descendants of immigrants until acquired by the Schwenkfelder Museum. (*See also* Figs. 51 and 199.)

51. Chest, painted softwood.
    H. 16¾ L. 50¼ D. 24¼
    Schwenkfelder Museum. Photo: Camerique.

52. Chest over drawers, walnut and chestnut with contrasting wood inlay.
    Inlaid, HN/1757/LR
    H. 25¼ L. 48 D. 22
    Privately owned. Photo: M. E. Warren.

This chest is said to have been found in Chester County and bears a
lock stamped with the name "Joseph Stumb" (*see* Fig. 35).[1]

53. Chest, tulipwood and white oak or chestnut.
Inscribed: 1764
H. 24⅜ L. 49 D. 23¼
National Museum of History and Technology, Smithsonian Institution.

The earliest group of Pennsylvania-German chests decorated by the same hand thus far discovered consists of four chests dated over an eight year period. Three have paneled fronts: two with dates of 1764 and one with the initials PW and the date 1765. The fourth chest has a solid plank front and the inscription CAD/RINA/1772/R. One of the 1764 chests (that at Winterthur) was supposedly found in Lancaster County. It and the example at the Smithsonian Institution are so European in style that wood samples of both chests were examined for more positive identification. Both chests were found to be constructed of American woods.[2] (*See also* Figs. 54–55.)

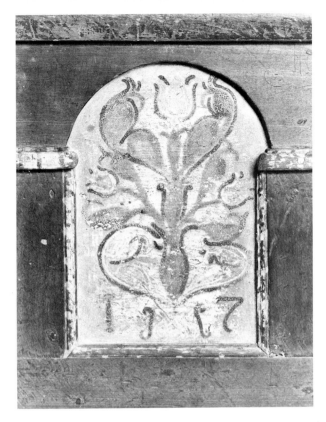

55. A detail of the left hand panel shows the crudeness of the brushed decoration (*below*). Photo: Meyers Studio.

54. Chest
Inscribed: 17 PW 65
Present whereabouts unknown. Photo: Meyers Studio, courtesy Mr. and Mrs. Jerome Blum.

56. Chest over drawers, painted softwood.
    Inscribed: 17A P65 [by finger painting in the two panels
    on the front]
    H. 27 L. 52¼ D. 23½
    Pottstown Historical Society. Photo: Meade A. Breese.

    The chest is said to have been made for Anna Potts, one of
    the daughters of John Potts of Pottsgrove.[3]

57. Chest, walnut with sulfur inlay.
    Inlaid: M 17 65 K
    H. 25½ L. 52 D. 24¼
    Mr. and Mrs. Richard F. Smith. Photo: Don Eckert.

    The turned feet are a conjectural restoration. This is the earliest known
    dated piece of Pennsylvania-German furniture with sulfur inlay. It was
    almost certainly made in the same shop which produced the Huber
    wardrobe and the chest shown as Fig. 208.

58. Wardrobe, walnut with sulfur inlay.
    Inlaid: GEORG HUBER/ANNO 1779
    H. 83 L. 78 D. 27½
    Philadelphia Museum of Art.

59. Chest, painted softwood.
    Inscribed: M W/P H/17 68
    H. 23¼ L. 49½ D. 21¾
    Mr. and Mrs. David Irons. Photo: Charles Hrichak.

    The decoration, though crude, probably pleased the owner of the chest.

60. Chest over drawers, painted softwood.
    Inscribed: ELISABETHA IODERIN 1769
    H. 28 L. 50 D. 23½
    Mr. and Mrs. H. L. Murray. Photo: James L. Dillon & Co.

    This chest may have been made in the Oley Valley of Berks County.

61. Chest over drawers, painted softwood.
   Inscribed: 17 S W 69
   H. 23¾ L. 41 D. 22½
   Abby Aldrich Rockefeller Folk Art Center.

Chests decorated with large hearts have most often been found in Lehigh County. This chest is the earliest of the type known. Another chest by the same hand, inscribed 17 CA PIN 70, is in the Barnes Foundation.

62. Chest, painted softwood.
   Inscribed: Jorg Jacob/Rex/In/Heidelberg/Anno 1769
   H. 20¾ L. 50 D. 22¼
   Mr. and Mrs. William Greenawalt. Photo: Richard Metzger.

The painter of this chest very kindly labeled it with the locale in which his customer resided, Heidelberg Township, Northampton (now Lehigh) County. He executed this chest for Jorg Jacob Rex[4] and another for Anna Maria L___?___ dated 1776.[5] Both have very deep (about 3") moldings cut from a single piece of wood at the base. Neither show signs of ever having had feet. (*See also* Fig. 204.)

63. Chest, painted softwood.
Inscribed: ADAM/ REISER/ 1770
H. 23 L. 49¾ D. 23
Tryon Palace Restoration, New Bern, North Carolina.

Only three chests have been located by this decorator who painted freely, but with a sure hand. His motifs are painted in black, white, blue, and red on a brown background. One chest was made for Adam Reiser (1770),[6] the second for Magdalena Helfrich (1775),[7] and the third for Madalena Herind (1783).

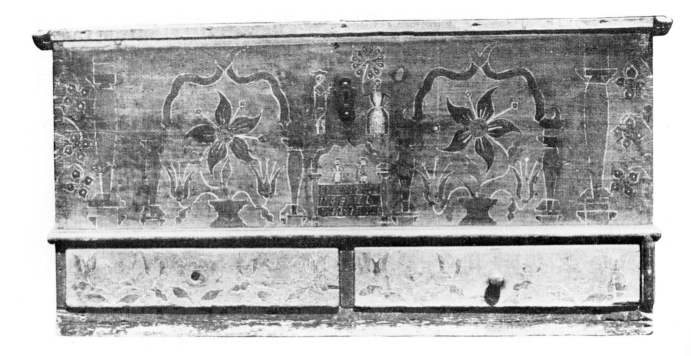

64 (*opposite*) and 65 (*above*). Front and one end of a chest dated 1771(?). The end design may be meant to represent two bell-ringing figures of the kind seen on European tower clocks. Reproduced from *The Pennsylvania Museum Bulletin* (November, 1925).

In 1925 Esther Stevens Fraser published the first of her articles on Pennsylvania-German chests.[8] In it was reproduced an important chest with a date she read as "1721." Since 1925 a number of chests by this same hand come to light and it is more likely that the date on the published chest is "1771." Unfortunately, as the style of our unidentified artist developed, the engaging human figures which appear on the early chests were discarded from the design repertoire. Only pots of flowers are found in the arched panels. Chests on which inscriptions can be read have the names of Georg Bihl (1782), Margaret Schumacher, Eva Dunckel (1786), and Rosina Dunckel (1791). The family names are associated with Berks County. (*See* Figs. 64–72.)

67. *Humpen*, a drinking vessel for communal use.
Possibly from Franconia, 1675
H. 10¾
Corning Museum of Glass, Corning, New York.

66. Chest, painted softwood.
Inscription obliterated.
H. 22 L. 50⅜ D. 22
Mr. and Mrs. Robert Zimmerman. Photo: Cal Pa

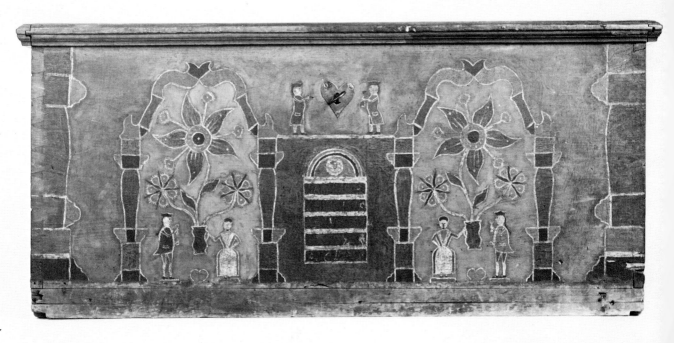

68. Chest over drawers, painted softwood.
Inscribed: Michael___?___DEN 19 DAIG/MERTZ ANO 1773
H. 29¼ L. 55½ D. 22¼
Privately owned. Photo: Camerique.

69. Chest over drawers, painted softwood
Inscribed: Eva/Dunckel/___?___/yahr___?___/den 19 avril/1786
H. 27¼ L. 50 D. 23¼
Metropolitan Museum of Art, Rogers Fund, 1944.

70. Chest over drawers, painted softwood.
    Inscribed: Rosina/Dunckelin/1791
    H. 26½ L. 50 D. 23½
    Privately owned. Photo courtesy Israel Sack, Inc.

71. Chest, painted softwood.
    H. 26 L. 50 D. 22
    David Pottinger.

    This painter of white outlines was fond of using motifs on a bare
    wood background.

72. Chest over drawers, painted softwood.
H. 25½ L. 49½ D. 21½
Reading Public Museum and Art Gallery.

The middle drawer of this chest is false. The bottom of the left hand
drawer is inscribed "Bode."[9]

73. Chest over drawers, painted softwood.
    Inscribed: Cadarina Brosiusen 1803
    H. 28 L. 49¼ D. 23
    Israel Sack, Inc.
    The pinwheel flower motif was used by an undetermined number of
    decorators into the nineteenth century. Two chests by this hand are
    known to have been made for members of the Brosius family.[10] The
    bracket on this chest is a restoration.

74. Chest, painted softwood.
    Inscribed [on the right end]: MRS AMELIA NEES/ COBURN/
    CENTER CO/ 1806
    H. 19½ L. 50 D. 20½
    Robert F. Nichols. Photo: Photo Optik.

The pinwheel flowers have lost their stems on this chest by yet another imitator of the original. The chest, which has also lost its feet,
was made or used in Centre County.[11] The inscription, in lettering of
a style inconsistent with the date, may have been added at a later
time. The rope handles are also a late addition.

75. Chest, painted softwood.
    H. 24½ L. 51 D. 22¼
    Belle Grove, the National Trust for Historic Preservation.

    Although once exhibited as from Virginia, this chest is almost certainly from Pennsylvania where others by the same hand have been found. The lid and feet are replacements.

76. Chest over drawers, walnut with pewter and wood inlay.
    Inlaid: 1773 H H
    H. 31½ L. 50 D. 23
    Privately owned. Photo: Triangle Photo Service.

    Although pewter has been found as inlay on a few Pennsylvania-German wardrobes, this is the only chest found so far using the material.

77. Chest, painted softwood.
    Inscribed: A.D.M.E./17 LW 74
    H. 21⅜ L. 50⅝ D. 23⅛
    Winterthur Museum.

Handsome woodworking and decoration almost monochrome in tone characterize the work of this craftsman. The "LW" may be his initials.

78. Chest, painted softwood.
    Inscribed: C.B.H.B./1776
    H. 24½ L. 50 D. 22½
    Yale University Art Gallery, Mabel Brady Garvan Collection.

This chest by the same hand may have been made for a married couple. The initials are probably those of two people with the same last name. The center foot is an unusual touch. The present foot is a conjectural restoration. Marks on the bottom of the chest clearly indicate that there was a foot in that spot.

79. Chest, painted softwood.
    Inscribed: 1774/MAR REY/DORS TEN
    H. 21½ L. 48 D. 24¼
    Pennsylvania Farm Museum of Landis Valley.

    Two of the three recorded chests by another artist bear painted bosses
    flanking the panels of flowers. These simulate in paint similar three-
    dimensional wood appliqués seen on Continental furniture. One chest
    is inscribed for Hannes Tommes (1774).[12] (See also Fig. 80.)

80. Chest, painted softwood.
    Inscribed: 1775
    H. 22¼ L. 48 D. 22¼
    Mr. and Mrs. Theodore Kurz. Photo: Geoffrey Clements.

81. Chest, painted softwood.
    Inscription on the front of the chest obliterated.
    Inscribed: [on the underside of the till lid] Peter Rohn hat das ge-
    macht/den 11 märtz Im Jahr/1784
    Present whereabouts unknown.
    Reproduced from *Pennsylvania Folklife* 9 (Summer, 1958).

The chest was probably made near Easton, Northampton County.

82. Chest over drawers, painted softwood.
    Inscribed: Cadrina 17/96 Sandern
    H. 28¼ L. 51 D. 23½
    Northampton County Historical Society. Photo: Jack and Jill Studio.
    This may well be a later piece of work by Peter Rohn.

83. Chest over drawers, painted softwood.
    Inscribed: 17 IOHANNES REICHERT 75
    H. 29½ L. 49 D. 24⅜
    Mr. and Mrs. Foster McCarl, Jr.

    The landscape with architecture is exceedingly rare on Pennsylvania-German chests, only two examples having been recorded. On both chests the buildings are obviously derived from renderings of European structures.

84. Chest, painted softwood.
H. 25½ L. 47 D. 21
Mr. and Mrs. Donald Wendling. Photo: Charles Hrichak.

Although frequently discussed in hushed tones as the "rarest of the rare," chests decorated with unicorns are not nearly so elusive as the mythical animal itself. Eighteen chests have been recorded, decorated with from two to four representations of the animal. In addition, there are another half dozen chests by the same artists lacking the beast in their decorative schemes. There are also about a half dozen miniature chests and boxes by these artists. The dates painted on the full size chests range from 1776 to 1803.

Fourteen of the most intricately decorated chests may all be the work of one painter. If not one, then there were two who were in close contact. They were perhaps two generations of the same family. Only three of the chests in this large group are inscribed with legible names and dates, those for Catarina Bruner (1784),[13] Heinrich Faust (1784),[14] and Margreth Bladt (1803).[15] The evidence points to an origin in or near Bern Township, Berks County. (*See* Figs. 84–85, 87–89, 91–96.)

The applied turned spindle on the back corner of the chest above is unique on an eighteen-century Pennsylvania-German chest. The feet are a conjectural restoration.

85. Chest, painted softwood.
Inscribed: 1778
H. 22 L. 50½ D. 23¾
Privately owned. Photo: Richard C. Carter.

The underside of the lid bears the stenciled name PETER DERR.

86. Chest, painted softwood.
H. 28½ L. 52 D. 24
Elizabeth Williams. Photo: Eugene Mantie.

As on the previous example there are five recessed panels. The pelicans or short-legged cranes in the end panels appear on no other chest.

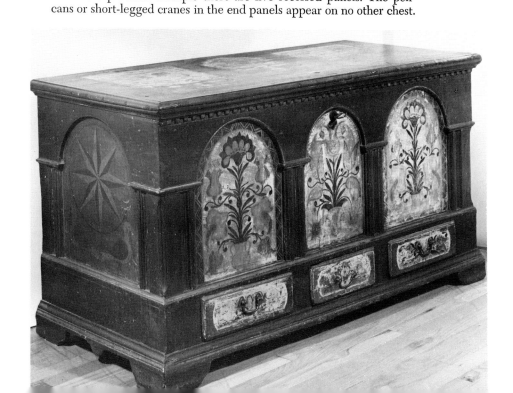

87. Chest, painted softwood.
    Inscribed: [center panel] A A
    H. 20¼ L. 46½ D. 20¾
    Stewart Frost. Photo: Triangle Photo Service.

    The initials must be those of either the owner or painter.

88. Chest, painted softwood.
    Inscribed: [on lid] 1784/Heinrich Faust
    H. 21¾ L. 50¾ D. 22¾
    Reading Public Museum and Art Gallery.

    Except for the lid, the color on this chest is very well preserved. (For
    a detail in color *see* Fig. 209.)

89. Chest over drawers, painted softwood.
    H. 30½ L. 53½ D. 22½
    Privately owned. Photo: Triangle Photo Service.

The lid, badly worn as usual, is also decorated with two unicorns between flanking panels of flowers. The crowned figure has metamor-
phosed from the cockscomb on the earlier chests.

90. The ends of the chest are handsomely designed and
painted.
Photo: Triangle Photo Service.

91. Chest over drawers, painted softwood.
Inscribed: [on the lid] Margreth Bladten 1803
H. 30½ L. 54 D. 22½
Philadelphia Museum of Art. Photo: Alfred J. Wyatt.

93. Painted wooden box, Alpachtal, Tirol, c. 1750.
    L. about 12
    Germanisches Nationalmuseum, Nürnberg.

    Friezes of painted animals such as these are also found on large pieces
    of furniture from the same general area.

92. Chest, nutwood with contrasting inlays, Swiss, early 17th century.
    H. 23½ L. 46¼ D. 22¼
    Schweizerisches Landesmuseum, Zurich.

    Since the unicorn in the left panel is paired with a rabbit in the right
    panel, we may assume here that we have symbols of chastity and
    fecundity.

94. Mangel, carved wood, Baden, dated 1737.
L. 23
Badisches Landesmuseum, Karlsruhe.

Confronted unicorns, rare in continental decoration, are here seen with parrots and with a hunting scene.

By Order of His EXCELLENCY

95. The British coat of arms, woodcut or metalcut on a broadside printed
    in Philadelphia by MacDonald & Cameron, 1778.
    Library Company of Philadelphia.

    This coat of arms appeared often at the head of documents in Penn-
    sylvania until the close of the Revolutionary War.

96. The coat of arms of Pennsylvania, woodcut or metalcut on a docu-
    ment printed in Philadelphia, 1782.
    Historical Society of Pennsylvania.

    This coat of arms first appeared in 1778, about the same time as the
    earliest known chest with rampant unicorns.

97. Bowl, glazed ceramic, German, after 1757.
    Inscribed: *Der alte Fritze komt*
               So batscht er auf die Hosen
               da läuft die ganze Reichsarmee
               u auch die Franzosen
               [Old Fritz comes
               He slaps his pants
               The entire Reich army runs
               And so do the French]
    Dia. about 13¾
    Badisches Landesmuseum, Karlsruhe

    "Old Fritz" is the Prussian king, Frederick the Great.

98. Side plate of a six-plate stove, iron, Shearwell Furnace,
    Berks County, about 1760.
    H. 23 W. 24
    Mercer Museum of the Bucks County Historical Society.

    The stoveplates may be the earliest use of the rider motif
    in rural Pennsylvania decorative arts.

99 (*above left*). *Exselenz Georg General Waschingthon*, by an unidentified artist, Pennsylvania, about 1780, pen and ink and watercolor on paper.
H. 8 W. 6½
Independence National Historical Park, Philadelphia.

The verse, in praise of various regional German foods, has nothing to do with Washington.

100 (*above right*). Birth and baptismal certificate, by an unidentified artist, Pennsylvania, about 1790, pen and ink and watercolor on paper.
H. 12½ W. 15⁷/₁₆
Privately owned.

One of the riders comments: *Ich iage nach der Crone der Gerech tig keit*
[I hunt for the Crown of Righteousness.]

There is no doubt that here the riders' intentions are of a lofty nature.

101 (*left*). Plate, glazed ceramic, attributed to Johannes Neesz, Montgomery County, about 1800–1825.
Inscribed: *Ich bin geritten über berg und dahl hab metger funten über all*
[I've ridden over mountain and valley—found girls everywhere.]
Dia. 12
Division of Cultural History, National Museum of History and Technology, Smithsonian Institution.

Lusty, rather than lofty, are the thoughts of the riders on ceramics.

137

102. Chest, painted softwood.
    H. 23¼ L. 47⅜ D. 22½
    National Museum of History and Technology, Smithsonian Institution.

    This chest may well have been decorated during the Revolutionary War years. The riders wear uniforms obviously closely patterned on those worn by Continental Army troops. The molding has been trimmed from the lid.

103. Chest over drawers, painted softwood.
    Inscribed: 1777/ANNA WEISIN
    H. 25⅛ L. 52¾ D. 22¾
    Mr. and Mrs. Richard Shaner. Photo: Andrew D. Bieber

    This chest is believed to have been made in Lehigh County.[16]

104. Chest over drawers, walnut with contrasting wood inlay.
Inlaid: 1·7·i 7·s·7
H. 30¼ L. 50 D. 25¼
Privately owned. Photo: Hayman Studios.

105. Chest, painted softwood.
Inscribed: [left pot] Christian/Selzer [right pot] Christ/ian/Selzer/
1777
H. 23¼ L. 52 D. 23¼
National Museum of History and Technology, Smithsonian Institution.

106. Detail of the right hand panel showing signature and date.

107. Chest, painted softwood.
     Inscribed: [center goblet] John Selzer/1804
     H. 24½ L. 52 D. 22¾
     Philadelphia Museum of Art.

108. Chest, painted softwood.
     Inscription largely illegible, but clearly dated: Januar/13/1800 [on
     the left pot]
     H. 22¼ L. 51⅝ D. 22¾
     Winterthur Museum.

     It is not certain whether this is a chest by John or by Peter Rank.[17]

109. Chest, painted softwood.
   Present whereabouts unknown. Reproduced from *Antiques* 11 (April, 1927): 281.

   The author of the original study of the Jonestown work presents this as a chest by "John Peter Rank."

110. Chest over drawers, painted softwood.
   Inscribed: [center cartouche] Jr 1788 Ao/Su Sa Na/Fihmennen [left and right pots] Michel Stoot
   H. 27⅜ L. 51 D. 23
   Reading Public Museum and Art Gallery.

   At this date the decorator could only have been inspired by a chest by the elder Selzer.

112. Detail of one of the horsemen with raised swords from
the Johannes Trump chest. (*See also* Fig. 207.)
Photo: Ronald Myzie.

111. Chest, painted softwood.
Inscribed: I · A · C OB · / · SCHA · RA · DIN · / · 1787 ·
Present whereabouts unknown. Photo: Courtesy David Stockwell,
Inc.

Three chests are recorded from the hand of one of the few decorators
to use carved blocks to stamp designs. Two of the three bear names,
this for Jacob Scharadin (1787)[18] and one for Johannes Trump
(1779).[19] The earlier chests are more elaborate. (*See also* Fig. 112.)

113. Chest over drawers, painted softwood.
Inscribed: Margreta Schmittin, 1779
H. 29 L. 49¾ D. 23
Mr. and Mrs. Irvin Schorsch. Photo: Camerique.

One or two decorators were active in producing one group of chests which always have designs in red and white on a green ground. Some of the chests have the initials "AH" in a circle painted in the center of the front. Chests are recorded for: Margreta Schmitt (1779), Jacob Jutszae (1781),[20] Johannes Bortner (1784), Magdalena Rausch (1790), and Margaret Lisbet Schmitt (1798). The family names strongly suggest that these chests come from upper Berks County. (*See also* Figs. 114 and 228.)

114. Chest, painted softwood.
Inscribed: MAR,GARET,LIS,BET SCHMIT,TIN, 1798
Present whereabouts unknown. Photo: Courtesy Photo Archives, National Gallery of Art.

115. Chest over drawers, painted softwood.
    Inscribed: GORG 17 81 BOSSERT
    H. 26 L. 47¼ D. 21⅜
    Mabel Brady Garvan Collection, Yale University Art Gallery.

    This is one of only two eighteenth-century chests which show the use of stencils. Both may have been made by the same hand close to the Berks-Montomery County line.[21]

116. Chest over drawers, quarter-sawed sycamore with sulfur and wood inlay.
    Inlaid: HEN.RICH MIL.LER/AN.NO 17.81
    H. 27 L. 55½ D. 23½
    Mr. and Mrs. Richard Flanders Smith. Photo: Don Eckert.

    Both the use of sycamore and iron drawer pulls make this chest quite unusual. It is almost certainly from Lancaster County.

118 (*right*). Wardrobe from the Hottenstein home, walnut with contrasting wood inlay.
Inlaid: DV AD/1781 HS [the initials are those of David Hottenstein]
H. 101 L. 91¾ D. 25¼
Winterthur Museum.

117 (*below*). Chest over drawers, walnut with contrasting wood inlay.
Inlaid: MARIA KUTZ/1783
H. 29¼ L. 54 D. 24½
Philadelphia Museum of Art.

This chest, with its most unusual inlays of grasshoppers, was found on the Sell farm between Kutztown and Bowers, Berks County. It is definitely by the craftsman who made the wardrobe with similar inlays found in the Hottenstein home near Kutztown.

119. Chest, painted softwood.
     Inscribed: Maria/__?__/1787/HS
     H. 21 L. 50½ D. 24
     Adele Earnest.

     This paneled chest with unfortunately worn decoration was definitely
     initialed by the painter. His "HS" is found in a small heart at the bot-
     tom of the center panel. Another chest by this artist is inscribed for
     Adam Grill (1785).[22]

120. Chest, painted softwood.
     Inscribed: AB HB/1787
     H. 24 L. 50½ D. 24¼
     Donald F. Seeger, Jr.

     The double set of initials may indicate that this chest was made for
     a couple after their marriage.

121. Chest, painted softwood.
    Inscribed: Elisabe: tha./Bamber gerj./Anno 1784
    Present whereabouts unknown. Photo: Courtesy Photographic Archives, National Gallery of Art.

    What appears to be a "j" at the end of the family name is a character signifying the two letters "in," the Germanic feminine suffix. A similar chest is also known to have been made for Johan Georg Wolfensperger (1784).[23] (*See also* Fig. 214.)

122. Chest over drawers, painted softwood.
    Inscribed: CH RIST 17 85 HA MA
    H. 26 L. 52 D. 23½
    Art Institute of Chicago.

    The six-pointed star over a pot of flowers was a design used by several decorators, including the one who made this chest for Christopher Hama.[24] The feet of the chest are missing.

123. Chest over drawers, painted softwood.
Inscribed: CA·DA/RI·NA/E·BER·H/ART·TIN/1·7·8·5
H. 29 L. 50 D. 23
Mr. and Mrs. David Mest. Photo: Meade A. Breese.

Decorated by the simplest possible means in blue and white on a
red background, this chest is probably from Berks County.[25]

125. Embossed and tinted parchment cover of a song book printed and bound in Germany for the Philadelphia bookseller, Ernst Ludwig Baisch, 1774.
Library of Congress, Music Division.

124. Chest, painted softwood.
Inscribed: MICHAEL CNODEL/ANNO/1786
H. 20 L. 51 D. 23¾
Mr. and Mrs. E. Clifford Durell, Jr. Photo: Charles Maddox.

The feet of the chest are missing. The design of flowers beneath an arch supported by Baroque twisted columns may have been inspired by a piece of European printing. (*See* Fig. 125.)

126. Chest over drawers, painted softwood.
Inscribed: 17 ELISABETH BINDERN 88
H. 28½ L. 50 D. 23
Privately owned. Photo: Helga Photo Studio, courtesy Ginsburg & Levy, Inc.

This artist, whose "trademark" is pairs of tiny flying birds, may have been working near the present Berks-Lehigh County line. (*See also* Fig. 216.)

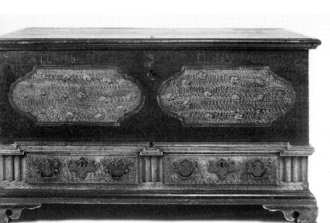

127. Chest over drawers, painted softwood.
Inscribed: ELISABETH REISTIN 1786
H. 27 L. 52 D. 25
Mr. and Mrs. Roland Jester. Photo: Savage Studio.

Very simple decoration in red and white has been applied to an outstanding piece of cabinetwork. The stepped molding is a most unusual feature of this chest, probably from Lancaster County.[26]

128. Chest over drawers, painted softwood.
Inscribed: Maria Stohlern/1788
H. 26½ L. 53½ D. 22¾
Byron H. LeCates. Photo: Hayman Studio.

The decorator of this chest, a painter of great capability and patience, was at work somewhere near Lancaster for about twenty years. He was fond of painting patterns of flowers and tendrils so like some of the needlework of the period that we could call him an embroiderer in paint. (*See also* Fig. 223.)

130. Detail of the capital "B" in the name Bahrt. The face sniffing a flower is delightfully whimsical. It is a motif that may well have been copied from a Fraktur. Photo: Froehlich Studio.

129. Chest, painted softwood.
Inscribed: Salme 1805 Bahrt
H. 22 L. 51¾ D. 22¾
Mr. and Mrs. Charles G. Frischmann. Photo: Froehlich Studio

131. Chest over drawers, painted softwood.
   Inscribed: Magdalena Leininger in Jahr 1788 Bern Township, Berks Caunty
   H. 27¼ L. 50 D. 22¼
   Privately owned. Photo: Camerique.

   Crudely brushed, the chests from the hand of another painter of unicorns are notable for their complex schemes of decoration. Two of the motifs used by this artist, the putto with a Liberty cap on a pole and the double equestrian figure, are unknown elsewhere in Pennsylvania-German painting. Three of the chests from his hand are inscribed with the names of owners and with dates—those for Magdalena Leininger (1788), Marichen Grim (1796), and Fritrich Heiser (1799). Two of the inscriptions also mention Bern Township, Berks County. (*See also* Figs. 132, 133, and 233.)

132. Chest over drawers, painted softwood.
   Inscribed: Mar.ri.chen. Grim. in Jahr 1796 den 10 febra
   H. 25½ L. 50¾ D. 23¼
   Philadelphia Museum of Art. Photo: Alfred J. Wyatt.

133. Detail of the two figures on
horseback on another chest by
the same painter as seen in Figs.
131 and 132.
Privately owned. Photo: Max
Hirshfeld.

134. The *Hochzeitszug*, detail from a
late medieval manuscript *Haus-
buch*, showing the newly wedded
couple returning from the ceremony with their attendants.
Reproduced from Eugen Fehrle,
Deutsche Hochzeitsbräuche
(Jena: Eugen Diederichs Verlag,
1937).

135. Chest, painted softwood.
Inscribed: Diese Kist Gehert Mir Abraham Brubacher 1788/J.F./
April den 22
H. 21½ L. 50 D. 21½
Mr. and Mrs. Richard Machmer. Photo: Donald Eckert.

Although possibly from the workshop of John Flory, the "J. F." who
signed this chest does not seem to be the same as that who decorated
the other chests attributed to Flory.

136. Chest, painted softwood, attributed to John Flory.
Inscribed: Diese Kist Gehert Mir Rael Hummer/Juni den 20. 1788/
JO FL
H. 21¾ L. 50½ D. 23
Privately owned. Photo: Max Hirshfeld.

137. Chest over drawers, painted walnut, attributed to Flory.
Inscribed: Diese Kist Gehöret Mier Rahel Friedrichin den 5/Ten
Augustus 1791
H. 27⅝ L. 56 D. 26
Present whereabouts unknown.

This artist is one of very few to paint on walnut. Both the parrots
and the crown on this example of his work seem to have been borrowed from the work of the well-known Fraktur artist Henrich
Otto.[27]

138. Chest, painted softwood, attributed to Flory.
Inscribed: Dise Kist Gehert Mir Veronica Ober/1794
H. 26¼ L. 50 D. 23
The American Museum in Britain. Photo: Derek Balmer.

139. Chest over drawers, painted softwood.
Inscribed: MARKRETA KUBER 1810
H. 27½ L: 47½ D. 21½
Dr. and Mrs. John W. Keifer. Photo: Howard Kraywinkel.

One of three chests which bear dates covering exactly a thirty-year period. All are either by the same hand, or the later two are the work of an artist copying the first. The design never varies. Chests were made for Catarina Brez (1788)[28], Markreta Kuber,[29] and Mary Schultz (1818).

140. Chest over drawers, painted softwood.
Inscribed: Margaret/Kernen/1788x
H. 28⅜ L. 50 D. 24
Winterthur Museum.

No decorator followed the example of Henrich Otto more closely
than the person who painted this chest, probably in Lancaster
County. Even the exact colors used by Otto on his certificates have
been copied. The lettering, however, is not like his. The feet are a
conjectural restoration. (*See also* Figs. 217 and 218.)

141. Chest, painted softwood.
    Inscribed: Abril den 13den Magdalena Ammin Ihre Kist 1789
    H. 24½ L. 50¼ D. 20⅛
    Mr. and Mrs. Matthew Sullivan. Photo: Richard C. Carter.

    This chest, with its five engaging baskets of tulips, may have been
    painted in Lancaster or in Montgomery County.[30]

142. Chest, painted softwood.
    H. 20½ L. 48 D. 21¼
    Privately owned. Photo: Max Hirshfeld.

    This is still another chest with motifs copied from the work of
    Henrich Otto, or from that by the so-called "Flat Tulip Artist," a
    Fraktur artist who followed him. The chest feet were probably
    turned and were set into square sockets cut into the underside of
    the chest. The base has a false molding formed by the projecting
    edges of the baseboards.

143 (*top*). The baskets of foliage in the front panels were copied from a drawing such as this one attributed to Henrich Otto. Philadelphia Museum of Art.

144 (*middle*). The lion on an end of the chest in Fig. 142 drawn in pencil and then painted. Photo: Max Hirshfeld.

145 (*below*). Chest, painted softwood.
H. 20½ L. 49 D. 18½
The New-York Historical Society

Most of the decoration was applied with a very free hand using a fairly wide brush. The bracket feet are missing.

146. Chest, painted softwood.
   Inscribed: Eva Catharina/Geigerin/1790
   H. 26¼ L. 50 D. 22¼
   Reading Public Museum and Art Gallery.

Of the three chests recorded by a decorator fond of checkered borders, only one bears a name and date: that made for Eva Catharina Geiger (1790). (*See also* Fig. 232.)

147. Fragment of a chest over drawers, painted softwood.
   Inscribed: ANNE : BEER/MARCH THE 18 1790
   H. 25 L. 50 D. 23
   Jean and Howard Lipman. Photo: Corbit Studios.

The bottom of the chest, with the feet, is missing, and the drawers have been removed. What appears to be unique paneled feet are really the two panels which flanked the drawers. Another panel would have been positioned in the middle between the two drawers. The chest is said to have been found in Slatington.

148. Stone designed to support an iron stove, middle Neckar Valley, Württemberg, 1787.
The upper part of the stone is inscribed: "Gerechtigkeit u Friede kussen sich" [Righteousness and Joy kiss each other].
Württembergisches Landesmuseum, Stuttgart.

149. Mermaids on a birth and baptismal certificate drawn for Sarah Ohnmacht by the artist "I.T.W.," after 1811, pen and ink and watercolor on paper.
13¾ by 16½.
[The child was born in Alsace Township, Berks County.]
Present whereabouts unknown.

150. Chest over drawers, painted softwood.
H. 25 L. 50 D. 23
Privately owned.

The drawers show no evidence of ever having had hardware. The artist probably resided near what is now the Lehigh-Bucks County line, and his work is characterized by scraggly, yet well-placed flowers. Similar chests are recorded for Johannes Gammel (1791), Jacob Schelli (1800), Elisabeth Weithknecht (1805), Elisabeth Merckel (1808), and Susanna Wittmer. (*See also* Fig. 237.)

151. Chest over drawers, painted softwood.
Present whereabouts unknown.

The drawer pulls have been replaced with sawed-off
wooden spools.

152. Chest, walnut with sulfur inlay.
Inlaid: 17 MARGARET ILGEN 92
H. 25¾ L. 52½ D. 22¾
Privately owned. Photo: Ronald Myzie.

Penciled inside is the inscription, "Remodelt 1857 by Benjamin
Hook," which explains the turned feet, so untypical of the 1790's.
Margaret Ilge or Illig lived near Newmanstown in Lebanon County.[31]

154. Chest over drawers, painted softwood.
Inscribed: [on lid] Susana Himelberger 1793
H. 29 L. 51 D. 26
Present whereabouts unknown. Photo: courtesy Ginsburg & Levy, Inc.

155. Wardrobe, painted softwood.
H. 85½ L. 88 D. 23⅞
Greenfield Village and the Henry Ford Museum.

153 (*opposite*). Chest, painted softwood.
Inscribed: [on lid] Valentin Himelberger
H. 23¼ L. 50½ D. 24¾
Dr. and Mrs. Henry Dyerle. Photo: Photographic Archives, National Gallery of Art.

A small group of elaborately-decorated chests and one wardrobe comprise the most European-looking Pennsylvania-German furniture. The cabinetwork is of the highest order and the floral decoration—daisies, carnations, and rather furry tulips—is painted with a sure and professional hand. Three of the chests bear the names of the same Berks County clan: Valentin Himelberger, Sibila Himelberger (1792), and Susana Himelberger (1793). The Himmelbergers lived in both Bern and Tulpehocken Townships.[32] An examination of the will of Philip Himmelberger shows that at least two generations of the family were craftsmen in wood. The chests bearing the names of the three Himmelbergers may indeed have been made by a relative.[33] (*See* Figs. 154, 155, and 224.)

156. Chest over drawers, painted softwood.
Inscribed: [inside the lid in pencil] Philip Zerbe
H. 27½ L. 50 D. 21½
Pastor Frederick S. Weiser. Photo: Budd Gray.

Another maker of chests, also probably working in upper Berks County toward the end of the eighteenth century, combined elements of design he had observed in the work of neighboring craftsmen. He used both pilasters outlined in white and floral motifs borrowed from one of the unicorn painters. His own touch was the sometime addition of little animals in the spaces outside the painted panels. Similar chests are recorded for Philip Zerbe[34] and for Stoffel Lebo (1794).[35] (See Fig. 230.) At the lower corners of the front of the chest above are figures of cats.

157. Chest, painted softwood.
Inscription obliterated.
H. 24½ L. 52½ D. 23¼
Metropolitan Museum of Art, Gift of Mrs. Robert W. de Forest, 1933.

The chest once had an inscription at the bottom of the panels. It has been very carefully rubbed off. The chest was probably made in Berks County.

158. Chest over drawers, walnut inlaid with contrasting wood.
Inlaid: 17 E L 95
H. 28¾ L. 49½ D. 23
Mr. and Mrs. Victor Johnson. Photo: Richard C. Carter.

159. Chest over drawers, painted softwood.
Inscribed: [on either side of the tops of the sunken panels] 1 7 9 5
Present whereabouts unknown.

This is the latest dated architectural chest recorded.

160. Chest over drawers, painted softwood.
   Inscribed: An: na: ca: ha: ri: na: Neu: in: 1: 7: 9: 7:
   H. 28½ L. 52½ D. 23
   Dr. and Mrs. Henry Dyerle. Photo: Photo Archives, National Gallery of Art.

   Four unicorns, two human figures, and two grotesques decorate this chest from the end of the eighteenth century. The family name of the first owner appears to be Neu.[36]

161. Chest over drawers, painted softwood.
   H. 29⅜ L. 51 D. 23
   Winterthur Museum.

   The capable artist of this chest seems almost certainly to have based his eagle design upon the bird which appears on United States coinage of the 1790's.

162. Reverse of the 1798 ten dollar gold piece.
Division of Numismatics, National Museum of History and Technology, Smithsonian Institution.

163. Chest over drawers, painted softwood.
Inscribed: GEORGE CORMAN 1818
Present whereabouts unknown. Photo: courtesy Bob, Chuck, and Rich Roan, Inc.

This artist, working at a slightly later date than that of Fig. 161, painted a much more Pennsylvania-German eagle; he holds two tulips rather than arrows and laurel leaves. Two chests by this artist have legible inscriptions, those for Wilhelm Waggoner (1813) and George Corman (1818).[37] The background of the chests is notable for the geometric tooling of the paint into arcs and six-pointed stars.

164. Chest, painted softwood.
     Inscribed: N S/Num 8/Sarah/Schuppin/Anno Christi .1.7.9.8. d 22
     Juni
     Philadelphia Museum of Art.

     The decorator who signed his chests "NS" also numbered them in
     sequence. Chest number 9 was decorated for Barbara Kunn in the
     same year. The artist may have worked in upper Bucks County.

165. Chest over drawers, painted softwood.
     H. 28½ L. 51 D. 22
     Mr. and Mrs. Robert Haska.

     The chest is of a type often found in Lehigh County and probably
     dates from the nineteenth century.

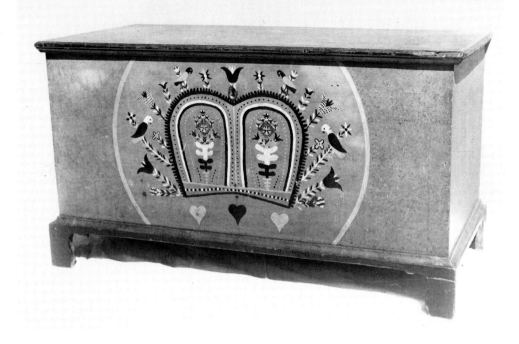

166. Chest, painted softwood.
H. 26½ L. 48 D. 23
Earl F. and Ada F. Robacker. Photo: Stephen Karas.

Probably from Centre County, the work of this artist is unusual for the disposition of the motifs around the large crown-like central design. (*See also* Fig. 243.)

167. Chest, painted softwood.
H. 24¾ L. 50 D. 21½
Winterthur Museum.

This is the only representation of Adam and Eve found on a chest, although the pair was very popular on printed broadsides. (*See also* Fig. 240.)

168. Chest, painted softwood.
   Inscribed: Eva Walborn/1804
   H. 22½ L. 51½ D. 23¾
   Privately owned. Photo: Max Hirshfeld.

The rare use of blocks to print an overall pattern distinguishes the work of this artist. He may have been working in either Dauphin or Lancaster County.

169. Chest over drawers, painted softwood.
   Inscribed: Ana Maria Lenkertin/1806
   H. 25¼ L. 49 D. 22½
   International Folk Art Foundation, Museum of New Mexico. Photo: Robert Nugent.

Of the six chests recorded by this decorator, four are inscribed with an owner's name and a date, those for Ana Maria Lenkert (1806), Christina Lenkert (1807), Michael Schäffer (1808), and Johannes Hoch (1808). The names suggest that the artist was working in the Lykens Valley or close to Bethel Township, Dauphin (now Lebanon) County. The designs vary little from chest to chest and are always in the same combinations of colors. The use of both a dull and a glossy black gives a very subtle quality to the decoration. (*See also* Fig. 238.)

170. Chest over drawers, painted softwood.
Inscribed: ABRAHAM 1805 KAUFMAN
H. 25 L. 50 D. 22¼
Mr. and Mrs. Charles Stroup. Photo: Max Hirshfeld.

Severely decorated, this chest and one made for Johannes Bahl (1799) are probably from upper Bucks County. The Kaufman chest lid is papered inside with pieces of a newspaper published in Milford Square, and the chests may have been made nearby.

171. Chest, painted softwood.
Inscribed: BAR BA RA
H. 19¾ L. 50 D. 22½
Present whereabouts unknown. Photo: Photo Optik.

Only rarely do Pennsylvania decorators depart from the use of panels to frame their designs. This chest, with a lid decorated with a grove of trees, is said to have been found near Harrisburg. The bracket feet are missing.

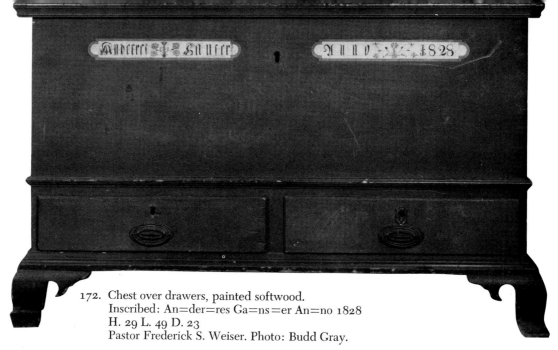

172. Chest over drawers, painted softwood.
Inscribed: An=der=res Ga=ns=er An=no 1828
H. 29 L. 49 D. 23
Pastor Frederick S. Weiser. Photo: Budd Gray.

Although the decorated chests of drawers of the Mahantango Valley are better known, a number of the older type of storage pieces of furniture were also made and decorated there. Working in the valley as early as 1810 and as late as 1828, one chest maker used only narrow bands of lettering against a dark grained background.[38]

173. Detail of the name panel from another chest in the same style, this one painted for Anna Maria Brosius. The Fraktur lettering is very carefully laid out in the panel.

175. Chest, painted softwood.
Inscribed: John Kesler den/16 Junius 1814/in Under Mahantango/ taunschip Schuhl Caunty
H. 23½ L. 51 D. [?]
Present whereabouts unknown. Photo: Photographic Archives, National Gallery of Art.

172

174. Chest over drawers, painted softwood.
Inscribed: Anamaria/Geresin den/11ten februarius/1812 In Mahantang/taunschip schulkihl/caunty
H. 23¼ L. 52¾ D. 18¼
National Museum of History and Technology, Smithsonian Institution.

A second Mahantango Valley artist used a much more elaborate decorative scheme and carefully labeled his chests as to place of origin.

176. Chest, painted softwood.
H. 23 L. 49 D. 22
Dr. and Mrs. John W. Keifer. Photo: Howard Kraywinkel.

A prolific craftsman who never inscribed his work with an owner's name or a date was at work near the center of the state in the first quarter of the nineteenth century.

177. Chest, painted softwood.
Inscribed: MADLENA/DEYNIER/1816
H. 25⅜ L. 53⅜ D. 23⅝
Dr. and Mrs. John U. Gardner. Photo: Dick Benjamin.

Small stamps in the form of circles and florets were used by another unidentified decorator working probably in Dauphin County. Chests are recorded for Jacob Zimmer (1811), Susan Kifer (1813), and Madlena Deynier (1816), as well as a number that bear only owners' initials.

178. Chest over drawers, painted softwood.
     Inscribed: MARY/BECHT
     H. 27¾ L. 50½ D. 23
     Privately owned. Photo: Geoffrey Clements.

179. A later chest by the same hand has a lid decorated with renderings of birds eating cherries. Photo: Max Hirshfeld.

180. Chest over drawers, painted softwood.
Inscribed: 1819 MARY BURCUP
H. 29 L. 50 D. 21½
Anne F. Hertford. Photo: Joe Deal.

181. Chest over drawers, painted softwood.
H. 24 L. 50½ D. 21½
Frederick Hanson. Photo: Photo Optik.

This chest is of interest for its lock marked by W. Clewell, who was working in what is now Monroe County, c. 1820. The feet of the chest are missing. (*See also* Fig. 36.)

182. Chest over drawers, painted softwood.
Inscribed: M. Kriebel/1823
H. 28 L. 50 D. 23
Jean and Howard Lipman.

The unusually fine lettering on this chest indicates that it was painted for, and possibly by, one of the Schwenkfelder Fraktur-writing family of Montgomery County.

183. Chest over drawers, painted softwood.
Inscribed: CHARL. 1829. SCHULS.
H. 27⅝ L. 49½ D. 21¾
Schwenkfelder Museum. Photo: Camerique.

Although by the second decade of the nineteenth century the old tradition of bird and flower painting was dying out, chests still carried the names of their owners. This chest was painted near Pennsburg, Montgomery County.

184. Chest over drawers, painted softwood.
H. 28⅞ L. 44⅜ D. 20⅜
Winterthur Museum.

This is one of the more eccentric forms of all Pennsylvania-German chests. It may date as late as the third or fourth decade of the nineteenth century.

185. Chest over drawers, painted softwood.
H. 30¾ L. 49¾ D. 22
Charles J. Kelly. Photo: Max Hirshfeld.

Of about the same period, and probably from York County, this chest has handsome orange graining and smoke decoration on the green drawer fronts.

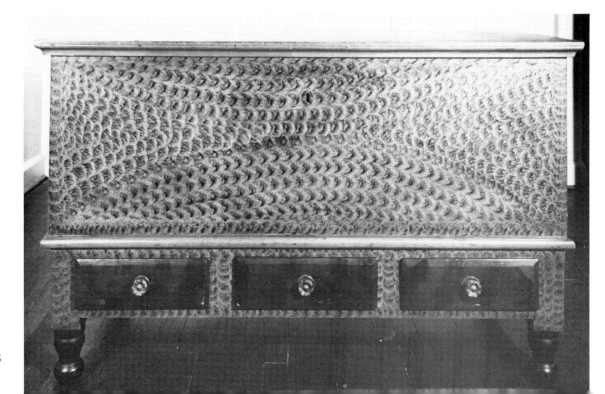

186. Chest, painted softwood.
H. 27½ L. 49
Present whereabouts unknown.
Photo: courtesy Samuel T. Freeman & Co.

Photographed when exhibited to be sold at auction, this chest is akin to the well-known Mahantango chests of drawers. The motifs are copied from printed documents circulated in southeastern Pennsylvania.

187. Birth and baptismal certificate, printed from blocks and filled in with pen and ink and watercolor, H. 13 L. 16, published by J. Hartman, Lebanon, 1818.
Rare Book Department, Free Library of Philadelphia.

The children on the chest in Fig. 186 are copied from woodcuts such as those seen on this certificate published in 1818.

188. Chest over drawers, painted soft-
wood.
Inscribed: Peter. Braun/1834
Present whereabouts unknown.
Reproduced from *Antiques* 10
(December, 1926): 427.

Only this one time does a hunting scene, so frequent on European furniture, appear in Pennsylvania. Peter Braun lived in the
Mahantango Valley. If the chest
was constructed in the same year
it was painted, the feet are a re-
markable example of *retardataire*
design. (*See* Fig. 7 for European
example.)

189. Chest, painted softwood.
H. 30 L. 49½ D. 23
Jean and Howard Lipman.
Photo: Corbit Studio.

Although this chest was published as being from Connecti-
cut,[39] at least two other chests of
the same design have been found
in Centre County, Pennsylvania.
A unique feature of the construction are the feet, the upper portion of which are fastened into
the inside corners of the box of
the chest proper.

190. Chest, painted softwood.
Inscribed: P G/1847
H. 24⅜ L. 45½ D. 21¹³⁄₁₆
Mrs. Harry L. Rinker. Photo:
Hayman Studio.

By the middle of the nineteenth
century the painting of chests in
the traditional manner was all
but a lost art. Those chests that
were made for use in rural Pennsylvania were generally decorated by paint graining or by the
use of stenciling.

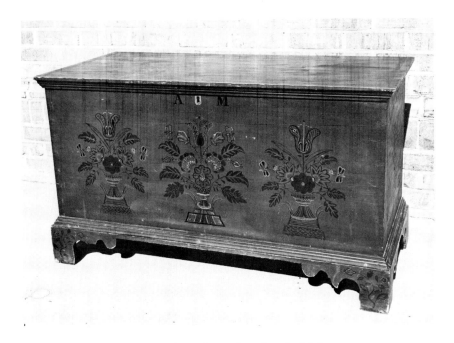

191. Chest, painted softwood, attributed to Joel Palmer.
Inscribed: [on the front] A M [on end] BUENA VISTA SIDELING
HILL
Present whereabouts unknown. Photo: courtesy Mary Bridges Vann.

192. End of the chest with the memorial of Buena Vista. Sideling Hill is near Needmore and the site of the Sideling
Hill Baptist Cemetery where Joel Palmer is buried.

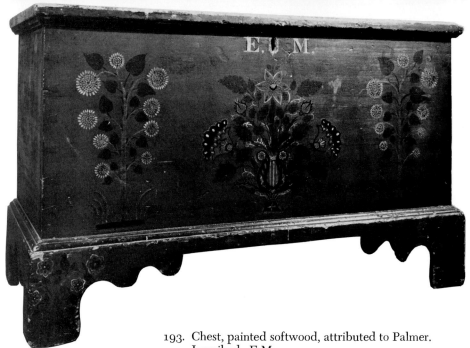

193. Chest, painted softwood, attributed to Palmer.
Inscribed: E.M.
H. 19¼ L. 31¼ D. 14⅞
Privately owned. Photo: Max Hirshfeld.
(*See also* Fig. 250.)

194. Chest, painted softwood.
Inscribed: M B 1854/Manu-
factured/By/Christian Blauch
H. 23¾ L. 43¼ D. 18¾
Greenfield Village and Henry
Ford Museum.

Painted and crudely brushed to
simulate veneer, the decoration
is all applied with the use of
stencils.

195. Chest, painted softwood.
Inscribed: LISSEE C BEANER
1877
H. 25¼ L. 37½ D. 20½
Privately owned. Photo: James
L. Dillon & Co.

196. Chest over drawers, varnished softwood.
     Inscribed: M K/1887
     H. 28½ L. 49⅞ D. 24⅜
     Mr. and Mrs. Charles K. Hall. Photo: Max Hirshfeld.

The chest is red with yellow drawer fronts. It bears a striking similarity to that drawn by Henry Lapp in his pattern book (*See* Fig. 197), even to the use of the same colors. It was made for Malinda Kauffman who lived near Intercourse, Lancaster County.[40] The four decals around the initials were added in this century.

197. Design for a chest in the hand-book used by the Amish cabinet-maker, Henry Lapp, working in Lancaster County, c. 1890–1904.[41] Philadelphia Museum of Art.

198. Chest over drawers, painted softwood.
Inscribed: M. B. Stauffer/1892
H. 27¾ L. 44 D. 22¾
Mr. and Mrs. Norman Kane. Photo: Meade A. Breese.

While the varnish graining was still wet, the name and date were
written with a blunt instrument or the end of the brush handle.

199. Chest, painted softwood.
Inscribed: Ao. 1732
H. 15⅛ L. 31¼ D. 16¾
Schwenkfelder Museum. Photo: Camerique.

This chest is believed to have been made and decorated in the cabinet shop of the *Unitas Fratrum* in Herrnhut. It was brought to Pennsylvania by the Schwenkfelders in 1734.

200. Chest over drawers, walnut with contrasting wood inlay.
Inlaid: ITI/1741
H. 29½ L. 48½ D. 20
Winterthur Museum.

By far the earliest dated chest with a tradition of having been made in Pennsylvania, an analysis of its woods has helped to support the assumption.[42] Both the front and the lid have elaborate inlay. It is said that this chest was made by or for Isaac Taylor, of Gap, Lancaster County. The cleated end lid is quite unusual on a Pennsylvania chest. The bracket may be a replacement.

201. Chest, tulipwood and white oak
     Inscribed: 1764
     H. 24½ L. 48¾ D. 22¼
     Winterthur Museum.

The "molding" at the bottom is actually formed by the edges of the projecting bottom boards. This appears to be the case with all four chests by this maker. (*See also* Figs. 53–55).

202. Chest, painted softwood.
     Inscribed: Johannes Jung. 1769
     H. 23½ L. 49¾ D. 23¼
     Mr. and Mrs. Arthur Sadley. Photo: Camerique.

The "toes" on the supports were carved long after the chest was made.

203. Chest, painted softwood.
   Inscribed: DEN 1 AUGUST 1773 CADARINA BOS/
      LERN BIN ICH GENANT WINSER/IST
      MEIN VATTERLANT DA BIN/ICH GAR
      WOL BEKAND CADARINA BOSLERN
      [August 1 1773 Cadarina Bosler I am named
      Windsor is my Fatherland Here I am very
      well known Cadarina Bosler]
   H. 24 L. 53½ D. 24
   Dr. and Mrs. Thomas Duane. Photo: Froehlich Studio.

   "Winser" is Windsor Township, Berks County. This is
   the only Pennsylvania-German chest recorded on which
   the bottom half of each hinge extends all the way down
   the back of the chest and half way underneath. The
   frieze of horsemen painted at the bottom is also unique.

204. Chest, painted softwood.
   Inscribed: Anna Maria/L_____?_____/In/Heidelberg/Anno 1776
   H. 20¼ L. 49 D. 22
   Mr. and Mrs. David Mest. Photo: Meade A. Breese.

205. Chest over drawers, painted softwood.
 Inscribed: CHR.ISTINA HEGERN 1775
 H. 27 L. 50 D. 22½
 Mercer Museum of the Bucks County Historical Society.

This chest with two patches of scraggly flowers was probably made for Christina Heger[43] in or near what is now Lower Milford Township, Lehigh County.

206. Chest, painted softwood.
 Inscribed: JORG/BREI/NIG 17/76
 H. 23½ L. 50 D. 23
 David Pottinger. Photo: Douglas W. Campbell.

Carefully designed and freely painted, Georg Breinig's chest was probably made in Lehigh County.[44] The painting on the end has a completely different character, being graining rather than figurative design.

207. Chest, painted softwood.
Inscribed: Johannes/Trump/1779
H. 23½ L. 50 D. 22
Mrs. Ursula Kempe. Photo: Ronald Myzie.

The chest is said to have been found near Zionsville, Lehigh County.

208. Chest over drawers, walnut with sulfur inlay.
Inlaid: [on the covering of the secret drawer beneath the till] 1783
H. 29¼ L. 53½ D. 26¼
National Museum of History and Technology, Smithsonian Institution. Photo: William Holland.

Said to have been found just south of Ephrata, this chest with "classical" motifs is one of the most important Pennsylvania-German pieces utilizing sulfur inlay. The chest is almost certainly from the same shop which produced wardrobes for Emanuel Herr and Georg Huber.

209. Right hand front panel of the 1784 chest made for Heinrich Faust
(*See* Fig. 88).
Reading Public Museum and Art Gallery. Photo: Meade A. Breese.

210. Chest, painted softwood.
Inscribed: [left pot] Christian/Selzer [right pot] Mille/Dubsin/1784
H. 22¾ L. 51¾ D. 22½
Reading Public Museum and Art Gallery. Photo: Meade A. Breese.

211. Detail of the center panel of a 1796 chest by Christian Selzer.
Winterthur Museum.

The design is one of the most unusual seen on a Pennsylvania-German chest.

212. Chest over drawers, painted softwood.
    Inscribed: [center pot] Johan/Rank/1790
    H. 25 L. 51½ D. 22
    Winterthur Museum.

213. Chest, painted softwood.
Inscribed: IACOB/RICKERT/ANNO/1782
H. 23 L. 53¾ D. 21½
Philadelphia Museum of Art, given by George H. Lorimer.
Photo: Alfred J. Wyatt.

This chest is said to have come from Lancaster County.

214. Chest, painted softwood.
Inscribed: Johan Georg:/Wolfensperger 1784
H. 21½ L. 48¼ D. 23
Historical Society of York County. Photo: Hayman Studio.

215. Chest over drawers, painted softwood.
Inscribed: ELISABETH DEN 22D/FRICKIN ANO 1785/ma ar
H. 27¾ L. 52¾ D. 24½
Mr. and Mrs. Victor Johnson. Photo: Richard C. Carter

The initials "ma" and "ar" in the lower inner corners of the two panels may well be those of the decorator. Decorated with parrots possibly derived from the birds which appear on a printed certificate circulated by the Fraktur writer Henrich Otto, this chest has the seldom-seen stepped construction.

216. Chest over drawers, painted softwood.
Inscribed: 17 ANAMARIA MVTHHART 86
H. 28 L. 48 D. 23
Mr. and Mrs. Eugene Elgin. Photo: Hayman Studio.

217. Detail of the chest painted for Margaret Kern in 1788 (*see* Fig.
140). The motifs and the colors are closely copied from Henrich
Otto's work.
Winterthur Museum.

218. Catharina Wächter's birth and baptismal certificate, printed in 1784 and completed by Henrich Otto in pen and ink and watercolor, paper, H. 13½ W. 17.
Privately owned. Photo: Eugene Mantie.

219. Chest, painted softwood.
H. 22 L. 51 D. 23
Mr. and Mrs. Eugene Elgin. Photo: Hayman Studio.

Another chest with flower form based upon Otto and with a most unusual six-panel design.

220. Chest over drawers, painted softwood.
      H. 27½ L. 49 D. 22
      Mrs. E. R. Hoover. Photo: Photography Unlimited, Inc.

      Not only is the body of the chest of stepped design, but
      there is a double dentil molding on three sides above the
      drawers.

221. Chest over drawers, painted softwood.
      Inscribed: 1788
      H. 30½ L. 50¼ D. 35½
      Philadelphia Museum of Art, Titus C. Geesey Collection.

222. Detail of the inscription on the chest made for Maria Stohler (*see* Fig. 128). The lettering is worthy of one of the better Frakturwriters of the period.
Byron H. LeCates. Photo: Hayman Studio.

223. Chest, painted softwood.
Inscribed: Catharina 1795 Mauren
H. 23 L. 52½ D. 22½
Privately owned. Photo: Hayman Studio

224. Chest over drawers, painted softwood. Inscribed: [on lid] Sibila Himmelberger 1792.
H. 28¼ L. 51¼ D. 26⅛   Winterthur Museum.
As this book goes to press, it has been determined that this piece
is almost certainly of twentieth–century manufacture.

225. Chest, painted softwood, attributed to John Flory.
Inscribed: Dise Kist Gehert Mir Jacob Dres/1791/JF
H. 25½ L. 50 D. 24
Philadelphia Museum of Art, Titus C. Geesey Collection.
Photo: Alfred J. Wyatt.

The most probable source of the unusual female head in an oval on
the Dres chest is a print published by John Coles. The portrait, of
Martha Washington, was published as a pendant to an engraving of
George Washington.

226. *Mrs. Washington*, drawn by Benjamin Blyth (1746?–after 1787), engraved by John Norman (c.1748–1817), published by John Coles, Boston, March 26, 1782, engraving, 13⅞ by 9¹¹⁄₁₆. The Mount Vernon Ladies Association of the Union.

Since John Norman also worked in Philadelphia for a time, the print that served as the model for the chest decorator may have been purchased there.

227. Chest over drawers; painted softwood.
Inscribed: Macht·da·le·na 1792 Lea·bel·sper·ger=
H. 30½ L. 53 D. 24
Privately owned. Photo: Geoffrey Clements.

The large heart motif was handsomely used by one decorator working in what is now the western portion of Lehigh County. He worked
there at least from as early as 1783, and chests by him are known
to have been made for Maria Keller (1784), Michael Finck (1789),
Machtdalena Leabelsperger (1792), and Johan Griesmer (1797).

228. Chest over drawers, painted softwood.
Inscribed: Magdalena, Rauschin, ANNO, 1794
H. 27¾ L. 50 D. 22¾
Mr. and Mrs. J. S. Heilman. Photo: Hayman Studio.

229. Chest over drawers, painted softwood.
     Inscribed: LUTWIG 1795 RAUB
     H. 28 L. 50¾ D. 22¾
     Mr. and Mrs. Eugene Landis. Photo: Charles Hrichak.

     This chest was made in Northampton County.[45]

230. Chest, painted softwood.
     Inscribed: STOFFEL/LE BO 1794
     H. 24¼ L. 50⅜ D. 22¼
     Reading Public Museum and Art Gallery. Photo: Meade A. Breese.

231. Chest over drawers, painted softwood.
Inscribed: 17 DANIEL EISZ 95
H. 28½ L. 50½ D. 23
Privately owned. Photo: Budd Gray.

232. Chest, painted softwood.
H. 25 L. 48 D. 22
The Virginia Museum of Fine Arts.

233. Chest, painted softwood.
Inscribed: Diese Kist Gehert Fritrich Heiser In Bern Tsh bercks
Caunty 1799.
H. 22¼ L. 49½ D. 22
Privately owned. Photo: Hayman Studio.

234. Detail of one of the two stars painted on the front of an undated
chest. Between the crisply lined points, the artist has finger painted
flowers.
Privately owned. Photo: Max Hirshfeld.

235. Chest, painted softwood.
   H. 20¾ L. 36½ D. 19½
   Privately owned. Photo: Camerique.

   Smaller in size than usual, this chest has boldly executed decoration.

236. Chest over drawers, painted softwood.
   Inscribed: 1804
   H. 27½ L. 50 D. 21¾
   Mr. and Mrs. Donald Wendling. Photo: Ken Clauser.

   Said to have been found in the Lizard Creek Valley in eastern Schuylkill County, this chest may actually have been made further south. Its affinity with earlier Berks County chests is obvious.

237. Chest over drawers, painted softwood.
Inscribed: Elizabeth Weithknechten 1805
H. 28 L. 50¾ D. 21⅝
Winterthur Museum.

238. Detail of the center panel of the chest painted for Ana Maria Lenkert in 1806 (*see* Fig. 169).
International Folk Art Foundation Collection, Museum of New Mexico. Photo: David Stein.

239. Chest over drawers, painted softwood.
H. 30 L. 53¼ D. 22¼
Mr. and Mrs. James Glazer. Photo: Chas. P. Mills & Son.

The sgraffito technique of chest decoration is not frequently observed. This chest, said to have been found in York County, was first given a coat of red paint and when that dried was overpainted in blue. While the blue was still wet, the fine scrolled design was scratched into the paint.

240. Chest, painted softwood.
Inscribed: MARY SHULTZ/1818
H. 23½ L. 49⅝ D. 22⅞
Mr. and Mrs. Malcolm McFarland. Photo: Camerique.

241. The unique appearance of a Biblical motif on a Pennsylvania-German chest is an engaging depiction of Adam and Eve. The chest from which this detail is taken may have been made in Berks County or further west in the Susquehanna Valley.
Winterthur Museum.

242. Chest, painted softwood.
H. 22¼ L. 51¾ D. 20¼
Mr. and Mrs. James Glazer. Photo: Chas. P. Mills & Son.

243. Chest, painted softwood.
H. 27 L. 50 D. 21
Peter Tillou.

One of a small group of chests of a highly individual character from Centre County. None of them is inscribed with an owner's name or date, but the source of the designs is certainly the Fraktur of Henrich Otto or the Flat Tulip Artist.

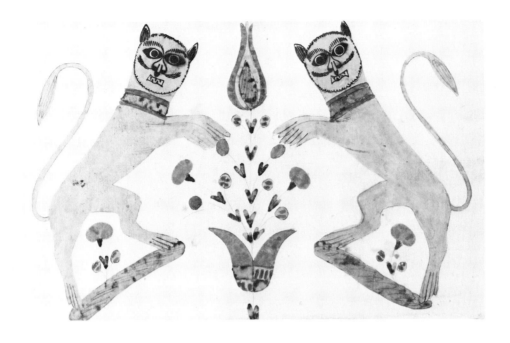

244. Lions and flowers, attributed to the Flat Tulip Artist, pencil and pen and ink and watercolor on paper, H. 8½ W. 13¼, c. 1800. Abby Aldrich Rockefeller Folk Art Center.

The figures of the lions are obviously traced around a pattern.

245. Chest over drawers, painted softwood.
Inscribed: Maria 1823 Kransz
H. 26 L. 48 D. 22¾
Bucks County Historical Society.

A fragment of bracket foot was attached when found.

246. Chest, painted softwood.
H. 26½ L. 51 D. 21¾
Privately owned. Photo: Max Hirshfeld.

The "house blessing" mounted inside the lid bears the imprint of the Allentown printers, Gräter and Blumer.[46] When the chest was found in Centre County, a piece of work by the Flat Tulip Artist was mounted over the left edge of the blessing.

247. Chest over drawers, painted softwood.
Inscribed: Sarah Hübnerin/1826
H. 28¼ L. 50¼ D. 23⅛
Schwenkfelder Museum. Photo: Camerique.

Made near Pennsburg, the chest is notable for its round panels. It was probably made and decorated in Montgomery County.[47]

248. Chest, painted softwood.
H. 24 L. 48 D. 20¾
Pastor Larry M. Neff. Photo: Budd Gray.

Decorated with large birds in freely brushed paint and stars and scallops in the sgraffito technique, this chest and another similar to it were found near Glen Rock, Codorus Township, York County.

249. Chest, painted softwood.
H. 27 L. 39 D. 18¾
Gerald Kornblau.

Paneled chests with corner members turned at the bottom to form the feet are very much in the English cabinetmaking tradition and are not often seen highly decorated. This chest, dating possibly from close to mid-century, was said to have been found in central Pennsylvania.

250. One of two sunflowers on a miniature chest decorated by Joel Palmer
of Fulton County.
Privately owned. Photo: Max Hirshfeld.

Notes to the Illustrations

1. The family name "Stumb" or "Stump" is not conspicuous in any Chester County records of the time, but does appear in Berks County.

2. By microanalysis, the lid, backboard, and bottom board of the Winterthur chest were found to be of tulipwood (*Liriodendron tulipifera*) and the face board of white oak. The Smithsonian Institution chest was found to have tulipwood in the lid, backboard, and bottom board also, and oak or chestnut in the face board. Oak is seldom found in furniture made by the German cabinetmakers of Pennsylvania.

3. This Anna Potts was born July 1, 1747. [Ms. family record at "Pottsgrove."]

4. This is probably the Jürg Jacob Rex who was confirmed in Heidelberg Church on the Third Sunday after Easter, 1765, by the Reverend Daniel Schumacher. He is recorded as having stood three times as a baptismal sponsor himself—August 14, 1766; March 11, 1770; and June 4, 1770—and each time with a different young woman as co-sponsor. [Frederick S. Weiser, "Daniel Schumacher's Baptismal Register," *Publications of the Pennsylvania German Society* 1 (1968): 387.]

5. In the inscription block the owner's name is badly damaged. It is fairly long and could be either Lautenschläger or Leibelsperger, both names associated with the Heidelberg area.

6. "Reiser" or "Rieser" are names found in Berks, Northampton, and Philadelphia Counties in the eighteenth century.

7. The 1790 census lists variants of the name "Helfrich" in both Northampton and Berks Counties. This chest is said to have been made for Magdalena Helfrich, born Sassamanhauser, who married Johan Helfrich in 1774. If so, it is an example of a chest decorated after the marriage. The couple lived in the Oley Valley, Berks County. [Information from the owners of the chest.]

8. Esther S. Fraser, "Pennsylvania German Painted Chests," *The Pennsylvania Museum Bulletin* 21 (November, 1927): 27–34.

9. The 1790 census lists a family named "Body" in the Maiden Creek Township of Berks County. If not referring to a family, then the word probably is a variant of the German *der Bode*, which merely means "bottom."

10. In the 1790 census the Brosius family is resident in Reading and in Heidelberg Township, Berks County. By the 1810 census most of the family were situated in Northumberland County.

11. The name "Nees" is indeed common in the area around Coburn, Centre County, in this period.

12. A drawing of the chest is reproduced in Frances Lichten's *Folk Art of Rural Pennsylvania* (New York: Charles Scribner's Sons, 1946), p. 96.

13. Formerly in the collection of the Metropolitan Museum, this chest was heavily, but expertly, retouched by the time it was sold at auction in the Stanley Todd sale [Samuel T. Freeman & Co., Philadelphia, May 23–24, 1966, item no. 76]. In the catalog the name was given as "Brumbrin." It should probably be read "Brunerin."

14. In the 1790 census four families of Fausts are listed in Bern Township, Berks County.

15. This is probably a member of the Plat family listed as living in Bern Township, Berks County, in the 1790 census.

16. The Anna Maria Weis for whom the chest was made is thought to be a daughter of Peter and Elizabeth Weis. She was born April 5, 1762 and baptized at Weisenberg Church, Northampton (now Lehigh) County.

17. The first research on the Jonestown painters was published by Esther S. Fraser under the title "Pennsylvania German Dower Chests," in *Antiques* in three installments: 11 (February, 1927): 119–23; 11 (April, 1927): 280–83; and 11 (June, 1927): 474–76. In the articles she conjectured that there was a Peter Rank, Jr. This seems not to be the case. It is possible that one of Rank's signatures was incorrectly interpreted.

18. The 1790 census lists families named "Sharadine" in both Longswamp and Maxatany Townships, Berks County.

19. The 1790 census lists a John Trump living in Montgomery County, the line of which is not far from Zionsville.

20. This could be the Jacob Judzy who was listed as "late of Bern

Township" when his will was probated at Reading, April 9, 1799. An inventory of his effects included "Two Bed and Three Chests—13: 10: 0." [Register of Wills, Berks County Court House.]

21. The 1790 census lists a George Bossart in Brunswick or Manheim Township, Berks County. The family name "Bosserd" is listed in Cocalico Township, Lancaster County, and the name "Bossert" in Montgomery and Berks Counties.

22. The 1790 census lists an Adam Grill living in Cumru Township, Berks County.

23. This is said to be the Johan Georg Wolfensperger who gave the land for Salem Reformed Church in what is now Campbellstown, Lebanon County.

24. The 1790 census lists a Christopher Hama living in Pine Grove Township, Berks County.

25. The 1790 census lists two households of Eberharts in Earl Township, Berks County.

26. The 1790 census lists four families named "Reist" and "Reisht" in Warwick Township and one in Lancaster Township, Lancaster County.

27. Henrich Otto (1732 or 1733–?) arrived at Philadelphia aboard the ship *Good Hope* in October of 1753 and signed the requisite entry papers as Johann Henrich Otto in his own hand. He was listed as twenty years old. By the spring of 1755 he was in the Tulpehocken and was evidently working as a weaver. By 1766 he seems to have been living in Cocalico Township, Lancaster County, where one of his daughters was born. Through his Fraktur he became a seminal figure in Pennsylvania-German art for decades. Although several chests bear decorations which are line-for-line his designs, they seem not to have been painted by him. On none of these chests is the lettering a match to that on Fraktur securely attributed to Otto. There is no evidence that Henrich Otto ever crossed the line between the crafts and decorated a piece of furniture. [Ralph Beaver Strassburger and William John Hinke, *Pennsylvania German Pioneers*, vol. 1 (Norristown, Pa.: Pennsylvania German Society, 1934), pp. 594–76; *Pennsylvania Berichte*, May 16, 1755; Birth and baptismal certificate of Anna Barbara Otto, Library Company of Philadelphia.]

28. Catarina Brez was born in 1768 and lived in Lancaster County until about 1827. The year 1788 is the date of her marriage to David Kinsey. She died in 1849 in Franklin County. [Information from the owner of the chest.]

29. A family named "Cober" is listed in the 1810 census as living in Mt. Joy Township, Lancaster County.

30. The 1790 census lists three families named "Aman" in Montgomery County. The chest, however, was found in Lancaster County.

31. Margaret Illig was born near Newmanstown, Lebanon County, January 31, 1774. She married Christian Reed on July 3, 1803, and she died June 24, 1842. The chest is still in family hands. [Reed Family Chart, Berks County Historical Society.]

32. When Sibil's chest was first published in Esther Stevens Fraser's "A Lancaster Pennsylvania Chest," *Antiques* 10 (September, 1926): 203–04, the family was erroneously placed in Heidelberg Township, and the chest was thought to have been made in Lancaster County.

33. "Item it is my will, that all my working tools, carpenters tools, and joiners tools, planes, chisel, gimbets, Saws, hatchets, and all tools, which belong to those trades, may Sons shall divide among themselves. . . ." [Will of Philip Himmelberger, November 28, 1790; Register of Wills, Berks County Court House.]

34. The 1790 census lists a Philip Zerbe living in Pine Grove Township, Berks County.

35. A Christoffel Lebo, with his wife Catharina, stood as a sponsor for Catharina, infant daughter of Peter and Susanna Hey at Host Church, May 11, 1809. The will of Christoffel Lebo, probated in November (probably of 1815) lists him as a resident of Tulpehocken Township, Berks County. [Church book, Host Reformed Church, Berks County; Register of Wills, Berks County Court House.]

36. The 1790 census lists a family named "Neun" in Oley Township, Berks County, and a family named "New" in Tulpehocken Township in the same county.

37. The 1810 census has a number of listings of the family name "Corman." Most are in Cumberland County.

38. Frederick S. Weiser and Mary Hammond Sullivan, "Decorated Furniture of the Mahantango Valley," *Antiques* 101 (May, 1973): 932–39.

39. Jean Lipman and Alice Winchester, *The Flowering of American Folk Art*, 1776–1876 (New York: The Viking Press, 1974), p. 238.

40. Malinda Kauffman was born in Lancaster County, December 31,

1866, and died there in 1902. She was married in the Amish faith in 1877. The chest was in the possession of descendants until 1977.

41. Beatrice B. Garvan, *A Craftsman's Handbook—Henry Lapp*, facsimile in color with introduction and notes (Philadelphia Museum of Art in association with The Tinicum Press, 1975).

42. The backboard, bracket foot, and the right rear foot block are black walnut (*Juglans nigra*). The bottom board and stretcher of the rear feet are tulipwood (*Liriodendron tulipifera*). The left drawer bottom is poplar.

43. On March 29, 1771, the Reformed pastor John Theobald Faber, Sr., confirmed a Christina Heger, age 15, at Great Swamp. On November 14, 1775, the same clergyman at the same place noted the marriage of "Georg Adam Dörr, son of the late Georg Dörr, of Old Goshenhoppen, and Christina Heger, daughter of Philip Heger of Great Swamp." [William John Hinke, *A History of the Goshenhoppen Reformed Charge, Montgomery County, Pennsylvania (1727–1819)* (The Pennsylvania German Society, 1920), pp. 470, 473.]

44. The chest was found near Breinigsville, Lehigh County. It was almost certainly made for either the George Ludwig Breinig who moved into Macungie Township, Northampton County (now Lehigh) in 1771 or for his son George who was born June 7, 1764. [Charles Rhoads Roberts et al., *History of Lehigh County, Pennsylvania . . .* , vol. 2 (Allentown: Lehigh Valley Publishing Co., 1914), pp. 145–46.]

45. Ludwig Raub was born May 21, 1772, in or near what is now Raubsville, Northampton County. The chest has remained in family ownership.

46. Alexander Augustus Blumer (1806–1842) and Augustus Gräter (1803–1863) seem only to have been in business together from around January 1, 1832, to January 1, 1834. [Alfred L. Shoemaker, "A Check List of Imprints of the German Press of Lehigh County, Pennsylvania, 1807–1900 . . . ," *Proceedings of the Lehigh County Historical Society* 16 (1947): 184, 205, 211.]

47. The Sarah Hübner for whom the chest was made was possibly the daughter of Henry Hübner (Heebner) and Anna Schultz Hübner, born January 30, 1808. [Samuel Kriebel Brecht, *The Genealogical Record of the Schwenkfelder Families . . .* (Pennsburg, Pa.: Board of Publication of the Schwenkfelder Church, 1923, p. 1232.]

Selected Bibliography

Bächtold-Staubli, Hans. *Handwörterbuch des deutschen Aberglaubens.* . . . 10 vols. Berlin and Leipzig: Walter de Gruyter & Co., 1927–1942.

Beer, Rüdiger Robert. *Einhorn, Fablewelt und Wirklichkeit.* Munich: Georg W. Callwey, 1972.

Bining, Arthur Cecil. *British Regulation of the Colonial Iron Industry.* Philadelphia: University of Pennsylvania Press, 1933.

————. *Pennsylvania Iron Manufacture in the Eighteenth Century.* Harrisburg: Pennsylvania Historical and Museum Commission, 1973.

Bramm, Otto. "Truhentypen," *Volkswerk, Jahrbuch des Staat-Museums für Deutsche Volkskunde.* Jena: Eugen Diederichs Verlag, 1941.

Bridenbaugh, Carl. *The Colonial Craftsman.* New York: New York University Press, 1950.

Candee, Richard M. "The Rediscovery of Milk-based House Paints and the Myth of 'Brickdust and Buttermilk' Paints." *Old-Time New England* 58 (Fall, 1967): 79–81.

Cummings, John. "Painted Chests from Bucks County." *Pennsylvania Folklife* 9 (Summer, 1958): 20–23.

Diffenderffer, Frank Reid. "The German Immigration into Pennsylvania through the Port of Philadelphia from 1700 to 1775." *Proceedings of The Pennsylvania German Society* 10 (1900): 1–328.

Fabian, Monroe H. "An Immigrant's Inventory." *Pennsylvania Folklife* 25 (Summer, 1976): 47–48.

———. "Sulfur Inlay in Pennsylvania-German Furniture." *Pennsylvania Folklife* 27 (Fall, 1977): 2–9.

Fales, Dean A., Jr. *American Painted Furniture, 1660–1880.* New York: E. P. Dutton & Co., 1972.

Fraser, Esther S. "Pennsylvania German Dower Chests." *Antiques* 11 (February, 1927): 119–23; 11 (April, 1927): 280–83; 11 (June, 1927): 474–76.

———. "Pennsylvania German Painted Chests." *The Pennsylvania Museum Bulletin* 21 (November, 1925): 27–34.

Garvan, Beatrice B. *A Craftsman's Handbook—Henry Lapp.* Philadelphia: Philadelphia Museum of Art in association with The Tinicum Press, 1975.

Gottlieb Mittelberger's Journey to Pennsylvania in the Year 1750 and Return to Germany in 1754. . . . Carl Theo. Eben, translator. Philadelphia: John Joseph McVey, 1898.

Harley, Rosamund. *Artists' Pigments, c. 1600–1835.* London: Butterworth & Co., 1970.

Hinckley, F. Lewis. *Directory of Historic Cabinet Woods.* New York: Crown Publishers, 1960.

Hollenbach, Raymond E. "Ausschteier," in the column " 'S Pennsylvaanisch Deitsch Eck," *Allentown Morning Call,* December 5, 1964.

——— and Alan G. Keyser. *The Account Book of the Clemens Family. . . .* Breiningsville, Pa.: The Pennsylvania German Society, 1975.

Hummel, Charles F. "Samuel Rowland Fisher's Catalogue of English Hardware." *Winterthur Portfolio 1* (1964): 188–97.

Hyde, Bryden B. *Bermuda's Antique Furniture and Silver.* Hamilton, Bermuda: Bermuda National Trust, 1971.

Kauffman, Henry J. *Early American Hardware, Cast and Wrought.* Rutland, Vt.: Charles E. Tuttle Co., 1966.

———. *Pennsylvania Dutch American Folk Art.* Rev. ed. New York: Dover Publications, Inc., 1964.

Langguth, Otto and Don Yoder. "Pennsylvania German Pioneers from the County of Wertheim." *The Pennsylvania German Folklore Society* 12 (1947): 147–289.

Lichten, Frances. *Folk Art of Rural Pennsylvania*. New York: Charles Scribner's Sons, 1946.

———. "A Masterpiece of Pennsylvania-German Furniture." *Antiques* 77 (February, 1960): 176–78.

Lipman, Jean and Alice Winchester. *The Flowering of American Folk Art, 1776–1876*. New York: The Viking Press, 1974.

Mercer, Henry Chapman. *Ancient Carpenters' Tools*. New York: Horizon Press, 1975.

Miller, Benjamin L. *The Mineral Pigments of Pennsylvania*. Harrisburg: The Topographic and Geologic Survey of Pennsylvania, 1911.

Montgomery, Charles F. *American Furniture, The Federal Period*. New York: The Viking Press, 1966.

More, J. Roderick. "Folk Crafts." *Arts in Virginia* 12 (Fall, 1971): 23–29.

Morse, John D., ed. *Winterthur Conference Report 1969: Country Cabinetwork and Simple Country Furniture*. Charlottesville: The University Press of Virginia, 1970.

Parsons, William T. *The Pennsylvania Dutch: A Persistent Minority*. Boston: Twayne Publishers, 1976.

Penn, Theodore Zuk. "Decorative and Protective Finishes, 1750–1850: Materials, Process, and Craft." Master of Arts thesis, University of Delaware, 1966.

Pilcher, James Evelyn. *The Seal and Arms of Pennsylvania*. Harrisburg: The State of Pennsylvania, 1902.

Ritz, Gislind. *Alte geschnitzte Bauernmöbel*. Munich: Georg D. W. Callwey, 1974.

———. *The Art of Painted Furniture*. New York: Van Nostrand Reinhold Co., 1971.

224

Ritz, Josef M. and Gislind Ritz. *Alte bemalte Bauernmöbel*. Munich: Georg D. W. Callwey, 1975.

Schiffer, Herbert and Peter B. Schiffer. *Miniature Antique Furniture*. Wynnewood, Pa.: Livingston Publishing Co., 1972.

Schiffer, Margaret Berwind. *Furniture and Its Makers of Chester County, Pennsylvania*. Philadelphia: University of Pennsylvania Press, 1966.

Schmidt, Leopold. *Bauernmöbel aus Süddeutschland, Österreich und der Schweiz*. Vienna: Forum Verlag, 1967.

Schlesinger, Arthur M. *The Colonial Merchants and the American Revolution, 1763–1776*. New York: Atheneum Publishers, 1968.

Shackleton, Philip. *The Furniture of Old Ontario*. Toronto: Macmillan of Canada, 1973.

Sieber, Friederich. *Bunte Möbel der Oberlausitz*. [East] Berlin: Akademie-Verlag, 1955.

Sonn, Albert H. *Early American Wrought Iron*. 3 vols. New York: Charles Scribner's Sons, 1928.

Strassburger, Ralph Beaver and William John Hinke. *Pennsylvania German Pioneers*. 3 vols. Norristown, Pa.: Pennsylvania German Society, 1934.

Tomlin, Maurice. *English Furniture, An Illustrated Handbook*. London: Faber and Faber, 1972.

Walters, Don. "Johannes Spitler, Shenandoah County, Furniture Decorator." *Antiques* 108 (October, 1975): 730–35.

Walzer Albert. "Baden-württembergische Bauernmöbel." *Der Museumsfreund*, vols. 8/9 and 10/11. Stuttgart: Württembergischen Museumsverband e. V. Stuttgart, 1969.

Weiser, Frederick S. and Mary Hammond Sullivan. "Decorated Furniture of the Mahantango Valley." *Antiques* 103 (May, 1973): 932–39.

Wust, Klaus. *The Virginia Germans*. Charlottesville, Va.: The University Press of Virginia, 1969.

Index

Personal names are spelled as lettered on the chests and as given in the sources, except that the feminine endings have been dropped.

Account books: Clemens family, 30–33; Abraham Overholt, 37; Peter Rank, 57, 65–67; Schmoyer family, 30
Adam and Eve. *See* Motifs
Adams County, 52
Advertisements. *See* Hardware *and* Pigments
Allentown, Pa., 56, 214
Alpachtal, 59
Alsace, 59, 84
Alte Fritze, 60, 136
Apprenticeship, 36, 66
Architectural chests, 42–43
Arnd, Daniel, 66
Aussteuer, aus steier, hausz Steüer, 28–33

Baisch, Ernst Ludwig, 150
Baltimore, Md., 67
Bänder. See Hardware
Batten, 41
Bavaria, 17
Bayrisches Nationalmuseum, Munich, 59
Beeswax, 51
Beilade, 40
Berks County, 34, 52, 58, 62, 114, 117, 144, 149, 151, 153, 162, 164, 207, 211; Alsace Township, 161; Bern Township, 128, 205; Tulpehocken Township, 29; Windsor Township, 187
Bermuda, 27
Bethlehem, Pa., 33
Birch. *See* Wood
Blacksmith, 37, 43, 44
Blauch, Christian, 64, 182
Block printing on chests, 62–63
Blyth, Benjamin, 201
Borstel, Kreis Pinneberg, 82
Bowers, Pa., 146
Bracket base, 41, 69
Brass. *See* Hardware
Breinig, Jorg, 188
Brethren, Church of the, 24
Brodhead, Rebecca. *See* Inventories
Bruderhaustischlerei, 26
Brushes, 58
Bucks County, 33, 57, 64, 161, 168, 171; Bedminster Township, 37
Butt hinge. *See* Hardware

Cabinetmakers/decorators: A. H., 144; Bachman family, 66; Blauch, Christian, 64, 67, 182;
Flory, John, 64–65, 154–156, 200; Himmelberger family, 162–163; Hook, Benjamin, 162; H. S., 147; J. F., 64, 154; J. T., 103; Lapp, Henry, 183; L. W., 124; Moravian, 69, 108–109, 185; Palmer, Joel, 64, 67, 70, 181–182, 216; Rank family, John, 65, 141, 193, Peter, 65, 141–142; Rohn, Peter, 64, 126–127; Selzer family, Christian, 64, 140, 192, John, 64, 141; Spitler, Johannes, 68, 104; Stoot, Michel, 65, 142; Taylor, Isaac, 185; Wilkin, Godfrey, 69
Cabinetmakers' output, 37
Cadet-de-Vaux, Herr, 57
Cambria County: Conemaugh Township, 67
Canada, 70
Carrying handle. *See* Hardware
Carving, 17, 50
Casein, 54, 56–57
Cash. *See* Contents of chests
Cedar. *See* Wood
Cedar chest, 27, 33
Centre County, 122, 169, 180, 212, 214
Certificates of birth and baptism, 35, 137, 179, 197
Chest of drawers, 26–28, 32, 37, 66
Chest-on-chest, 26–27
Chester, Pa., 47
Chester County, 109
Chestnut. *See* Wood
Chippendale, Thomas, 26, 85
Clemens family account book. *See* Account books
Clewell, W., 100, 176
Coat of arms: British, 59–60, 135; Commonwealth of Pennsylvania, 59–60, 135
Coles, John, 200–201
Colors. *See* Pigments
Combs, 58
Continental Congress, First, 48
Construction, 38–43
Contents of chests: cash, 35; clothes, 16, 21, 24–25, 34; food, 16, 21, 34; linens, 16, 29, 34–35; quilts, 33; tools, 34
Corn cobs, 58

Dauphin County, 170, 174; Bethel Township, 64, 170
Deckelkästchen, 40
Decoration, techniques of. *See:* Carving, Inlay *and* Painting
Dodderer, Veronica. *See* Inventories
Dovetailing, 27, 38–39
Dowels, 16–17, 39–41
Dower chest, 28
Dowry, 29, 31
Draar, Traar, Trar, 32
Drawers, 27, 39–40

Drog, Trog, 15

Easton, Pa., 64, 126
Ephrata, Pa., 190
Escutcheon. *See* Hardware
European origins of chests, 15–18

Factory-made furniture, 71
Feathers, 58
Feet, 17, 40–41
Finishes: shellac, 52, 63; varnish, 52, 63. *See also* Paint
Fisher, Joshua & Son, 48
Fisher, Samuel Rowland, 48
Flat Tulip Artist, 158, 212–213
Flory, John, 64–65, 154–156, 200
Fraktur, 35, 61
Fraktur writers. *See* Flat Tulip Artist, Henrich Otto, *and* Friederich Speyer
Franconia, 118
Frankfurt, Germany, 19
Fraser, Esther Stevens, 117
Frederick, Md., 68, 103
Frederick the Great, 60–61, 136
Frontalstollentruhe. See Truhe
Fulton County, 216; Belfast Township, 67
Furniture-making families. *See* Cabinet makers/ decorators

Gap, Pa., 185
Germantown, Pa., 18, 20
Glass knobs. *See* Hardware
Glen Rock, Pa., 215
Graining, 57–58
Gremer, Jacop, 66
Gräter and Blumer, 214
Groh, John, 66
Guilds, 16, 36

Hancock, Md., 67
Hardware: advertisements for, 43–45, 47–48; *bänder,* 31, 44; brass knobs, 49; butt hinges, 44; carrying handles, 43–45; drawer pulls, 43, 47–49; escutcheons, 43; filed edges of, 45–46; glass knobs, 49; H and HL hinges, 44; *hand-haben,* 44; hinges, 43–44; keyhole guards, 47–49; keys, 47; locks, 43, 46; nails, 41, 45; porcelain knobs, 49; rivets, 45; *schlosz,* 31; *schwalben schwanz-bänder,* 44; screws, 46, 49; swallowtail hinges, 44
Hardwood, 16–17. *See also* Wood
Harrisburg, Pa., 171
Hartman, J., 179
Henry Francis du Pont Winterthur Museum, 48, 50–51, 65
Herr, Emanuel, 190
Hermhut, Saxony, 26
Himmelberger, Phillip. *See* Wills
Hochzeitszug, 61, 154

Holland, 53
Holly. *See* Wood
Hook, Benjamin, 162
Hope chest, 33
Hörner, Johann Phillip, 19
Hottenstein, David, 146
Huber, Georg, 190

Immigrants and immigration, 18–23, 25
Indiana, 70, 107
Inlay: pewter, 50–51; putty, 69; sulfur, 38, 51; wood, 38; white wax, 51
Intercourse, Pa., 183
Inventories, quotes from: Brodhead, Rebecca, 34; Clemens family, 30–33; Dodderer, Veronica, 35; Jacobs, Barbara, 35; Keyser, Lucina, 24–25; Moyer, Abraham, 34; Moyer, Casper, 34; Myer, Abraham, 61; Rösli, Conrad, 34; Selzer, John, 65; Smith, Henry, 35; Wentz, Elizabeth, 34; Yotter, Abraham, 35
Ipswich, Mass., 52
Iron. *See* Hardware
Iron manufacture, 43–44

Jacobs, Barbara. *See* Inventories
Jonestown, Pa., 64–65, 68

Kammer, 16, 33
Kassel, 83
Kasten, 15
Kastentruhe. See Truhe
Kauffman, Henry, 47
Keys. *See* hardware
Keyhole plates. *See* Hardware
Keyser, Lucina. *See* Inventories
Kischt, Kist, Kiste, 15, 18, 32, 42
Kleider Shank, 32
Knobs. *See* Hardware
Krauss, Johann, 56–57
Krips, Philip, 66
Kutztown, Pa., 146

Lade, Lade in der Lade, 40
Lancaster, Pa., 36, 51, 53, 61
Lancaster County, 52, 64, 145, 151, 157, 158, 170, 183, 185, 194; Rapho Township, 64
Lebanon County, 29, 57; Bethel Township, 170
Lehigh County, 52, 115, 138, 151, 161, 188, 189, 202; Heidelberg Township, 115, 187; Lower Macungie Township, 115, 187; Lower Milford Township, 188
Lids, 15, 41
Lion. *See* Motifs
Lizard Creek Valley, 207
Location of chests in homes, 34
Locks. *See* Hardware
London, 53, 55
Lownes, Caleb, 60
Lykens Valley, 170

Maal, Thomas, 43
MacDonald & Cameron, 135
Mahantango Valley, 172–173
Manheim, Pa., 64
Maple. *See* Wood
Marriage gift. *See Aussteuer*
Marshall, Christopher, 52
Maryland, 67–68
Maytown, Pa., 64
Measurements of chests, 39
M'Elwee, John, 55
Mennonites, 30, 33
Mermaid. *See* Motifs
Milford Square, Pa., 171
Milk-base paint, 56–57
Mineral pigment deposits. *See* Pigments
Mink, George, 66
Mittelberger, Gottlieb, 36
Molding, 39–42
Monroe County, 176
Montgomery, Charles, 51
Montgomery County: Frederick Township, 35; Providence Township, 34; Salford Township, 30; Skippack Township, 35; Upper Hanover Township, 35, Worcester Township, 34
Moravians, 26, 69
Morris, Gov. Robert Hunter, 20, 24
Motifs, 58–62: Adam and Eve, 169, 211; double equestrian figures, 61; eagle, 166–167; horse and rider, 60–61; kneeling children, 179; lion, 60; mermaid, 61–62; toasting man and woman, 58–59; unicorn, 59–60
Moyer, Abraham. *See* Inventories
Moyer, Casper. *See* Inventories
Mt. Joy, Pa., 64
Museum für Deutsche Volkskunde, Berlin, 25
Myer, Abraham. *See* Inventories
Mule chest, 27

Needmore, Pa., 67
Neesz, Johannes, 137
Neuenburg, Canton, Switzerland, 70
Newspaper advertisements. *See* Hardware *and* Pigments
Nixe. See Motifs: mermaid
Non-importation policy, 48
Norman, John, 201
North Carolina, 67, 69
Northampton County, 52; Lower Saucon Township, 34; Upper Milford Township, 24
Numbered chests, 68, 168

Oak. *See* Wood
Oeconomisches Haus-und Kunst-Buch, 56
Ogee foot. *See* Feet
Ohio, 67–68, 70
Ohnmacht, Sarah, 161
Oil as paint vehicle, 53, 56–57

Oley Valley, 33, 61
Original owners of chests: Ammin, Magdalena, 158; Badrof, Susana, 64; Bahl, Johannes, 171; Bahrt, Salme, 152; Bamberger, Elisabe., 148; Beaner, Lissee, 82; Becht, Mary, 175; Beer, Anne, 160; Bihl, Georg, 117; Binder, Elisabeth, 151; Bladt, Margreth, 128, 132; Bortner, Johannes, 144; Bosler, Cadarina, 187; Bossert, Gorg, 145; Braun, Peter, 180; Brez, Catarina, 156; Brosius, Anna Maria, 172; Brosius, Cadarina, 128; Burcup, Mary, 176; Cnodel, Michael, 150; Corman, George, 167; Derr, Peter, 129; Deynier, Madlena, 174; Dorst, Marrey, 125; Dres, Jacob, 64, 200; Dubs, Mille, 192; Dunckel, Eva, 117, 119; Dunckel, Rosina, 117, 120; Eberhartt, Cadarina, 149; Eisz, Daniel, 204; Faust, Heinrich, 128, 130, 191; Fihmenn, Susana, 142; Finck, Michael, 202; Frick, Elisabeth, 195; Friedrich, Rahel, 64, 155; Gammel, Johannes, 161; Ganser, Anderres, 172; Geiger, Eva Catharina, 160; Geres, Anamaria, 173; Griesmer, Johan, 202; Grill, Adam, 147; Grim, Marrichen, 60, 153; Hama, Christ., 148; Heger, Christina, 188; Heiser, Fritrich, 153, 205; Helfrich, Magdalena, 116; Herind, Madalena, 116; Himmelberger, Sibila, 163, 200; Himelberger, Susana, 163; Himelberger, Valentin, 162–163; Hirschy, Philip, 70, 107; Hoch, Johannes, 170; Hübner, Sarah, 214; Hummer, Rael, 64, 155; Ioder, Elisabetha, 114; Ilge, Margaret, 162; Jung, Johannes, 186; Jutszae, Jacob, 144; Kauffman, Malinda, 183; Kaufman, Abraham, 171; Keller, (Se)bastian, 64; Keller, Maria, 202; Kern, Margaret, 157, 196; Kesler, John, 172; Kifer, Susan, 174; Kranz, Maria, 213; Kriebel, M., 177; Kuber, Markreta, 156; Kunn, Barbara, 168; Kutz, Maria, 146; Leabelsperger, Machtdalena, 202; Lebo, Stoffel, 203; Leininger, Magdalena, 153; Lenkert, Ana Maria, 170, 209; Lenkert, Christina, 170; Maur, Catharina, 199; Merckel, Elisabeth, 161; Miller, Henrich, 145; Muthhart, Ana Maria, 195; Nees, Amelia, 122; Neff, Adam, 103; Neu, Anna Caharina, 166; Ober, Veronica, 64, 157; Potts, Anna, 112; Raub, Lutwig, 63, 203; Rausch, Magdalena, 144, 202; Reichert, Johannes, 127; Reiser, Adam, 116; Reist, Elisabeth, 151; Rex, Jorg Jacob, 115; Rickert, Daniel, 64; Rickert, Jacob, 194; Sander, Cadrina, 127; Schäffer, Michael, 170; Scharadin, Jacob, 143; Schelli, Jacob, 161; Schmitt, Margreta, 144; Schmitt, Margaret Lisbet, 144; Schneider, Pedras, 64; Schuls, Charl., 177; Shultz, Mary, 156, 210; Schumacher, Margaret, 117; Schupp, Sarah, 168; Stauffer, M. B., 184; Stohler, Maria, 151, 199; Taylor, Isaac, 185, Tommes, Hannes, 125; Trump, Johannes,

143, 189; Waggoner, Wilhelm, 167; Walborn, Eva, 170; Wesi, Anna, 138; Weithknecht, Elizabeth, 161, 208; Witmer, Maria, 64; Wittmer, Susanna, 161; Wolfensperger, Johan Georg, 148, 194; Zerbe, Philip, 164; Zimmer, Jacob, 174
Otto, Henrich, 195–197
Overholt, Abraham, 37, 57

Paint, 52–58. *See also* Casein, Milk-base paint *and* Pigments
Paint, ready-mixed, 56
Painting, 17–18, 37, 57–58, 66
Palatinate, 16
Palmer, Joel, 64, 67, 70, 181–182, 216
Pastorius, Francis Daniel, 18
Patterns, 62
Pennsylvania: Assembly, 48; Provincial Council, 18; State Archives, 19.
Pennsylvania Journal, 53
Personal property, chests as, 28
Peters, James, 53–5
Philadelphia, Pa., 19, 43, 48–49, 52–53, 55, 60
Philadelphia Museum of Art, 50
Picture frame, chest as, 35
Pigments: advertisements for, 52–53; mineral deposits of, 52; Brunswick green, 55; cadmium yellow, 56; carmine, 55; chrome yellow, 55; cobalt blue, 55; emerald green, 55; flake white, 53; ivory black, 54; lampblack, 54; lake, 55; massicot, 55; ochre, 54; Patent yellow, 55; Prussian blue, 54; red lead, 53; sienna, 55; smalt, 54; Spanish brown, 53; ultramarine, 54; umber, 54; verdigrise, 54; vermilion, 53; white lead, 53; yellow ochre, 55
Pilasters, 42
Plundering of chests, 20–24
Pine. *See* Wood
Polar. *See* Wood
Porcelain knobs. *See* Hardware
Portsmouth, N.H., 52
Prices of chests, 25, 31–32, 37, 66

Quilts. *See* Contents of chests

Rätisches Museum, Chur, Switzerland, 59
Rahn, Peter. *See* Rohn, Peter
Rank family: Daniel, 66; John, 65, 193; Peter, 65–67, 141–142; Peter Rank account book, 57, 65–67, Sarah, 65
Repertory of Arts and Manufactures, The, 57
Richardson, Francis, 48
Ritz, Gislind, 56
Rivet. *See* Hardware
Rohn, Peter, 64, 126–127
Rösli, Conrad. *See* Inventories
Runners, 17, 40–41

Sauer, Christopher, 20–23, 33, 60
Saxony, 26
Schleswig-Holstein, 81
Schlosz. See Hardware
Schmoyer family account book. *See* Account books
Schuylkill County, 207; Mahantango Township, 173; Under Mahantango Township, 172
Schwalbenschwanz-bänder. See Hardware
Schweizerisches Landsmuseum, Zurich, 59
Schwenkfelders, 25
Schwenkfelder Museum, Pennsburg, Pa., 25
Screws. *See* Hardware
Secret drawer, 40
Seitstollentruhe. See Truhe
Sell farm, Berks County, 146
Selzer family: Christian, 62, 65, 140, 192; Christian, Jr., 65; John, 65, 141
Sensebezirk, 88
Shearwell Furnace, 61
Shellac. *See* Finishes
Shenandoah Valley, 68
Shonk (Schrank), 15, 59
Shoufler, Valentine, 66
Sideling Hill Baptist Cemetery, 181
Signed hardware, 47
Simmerman, Mikkele, 66
Slatington, Pa., 160
Smith, Henry. *See* Inventories
Smithsonian Institution, 61
Sockel, 17
Softwood, 16–17, 25. *See also* Wood
Somerset County, 67
Speyer, Friederich, 86
Stencils, 17, 63
Stepns, Richert, 66
Stepped profile of chests, 40
Stollentruhe. See Truhe
Stoot, Michel, 65, 142
Stow, John, 48
Streater, Robert, 47
String in chests, 35
Stube, 16
Stumb, Joseph, 99, 109
Sulfur inlay. *See* Inlay
Supports. *See* Bracket base, Feet, *Sockel* and Runners
Susquehanna Valley, 211
Swallowtail hinges. *See* Hardware
Switzerland, 49, 59, 82, 84, 88
Sycamore. *See* Wood

Tacks. *See* Hardware
Templates, 62
Till, 35, 40
Tirol, 59, 81
Tongue-and-groove, 38
Tools, 37, 38
Truhe, 15; *Frontalstollen-,* 17; *Kasten-,* 17; *Stollen-,*

16, 17; *Seitstollen-*, 17.
Tulip poplar. *See* Wood
Turner, James, 55

Unicorn. *See* Motifs
Unitas Fratrum, 26, 69

Varnish. *See* Finishes
Veneer, 18, 70
Virginia, 67, 68; Hardy County, 68; Shenandoah
    County; Wythe County, 68
Vockenrath, Germany, 19

Wächter, Catharina, 197
Walnut. *See* Wood
Walporn, Make lena, 66
Wardrobe, 15, 31, 32, 50–51. *See also Shonk*
Washington, George, 61, 137, 200
Washington, Martha, 200–201
Wassergeist, 62
Wedding procession, 61, 154
Wentz, Elizabeth. *See* Inventories
Wertheim, 24
West Virginia, 69; Hardy County, 69
Wetherill, Samuel, 53
White lead, 51
White wax. *See* Inlay
Whitewash, 54
Wilkin, Godfrey, 69
Wills, quotes from: Phillip Himmelberger, 29;
    Christian Selzer, Jr., 65; John George Wolfes-
    barger, 29–30
Wilson, Andey, 66
Winterthur. *See* Henry Francis du Pont Winterthur
    Museum
Wolfesbarger, John George. *See* Wills
Wood: birch, 51; cedar, 27; chestnut 38; holly, 51;
    maple, 51; oak, 16, 38; pine, 25, 31–32, 37–
    38, 69; poplar, 37; sycamore, 50; tulip poplar,
    37; walnut, 31–32, 37–38, 50–51
Wood, thickness of, 38–39
Württemberg, 68, 83

Yoder, Elisabeth, 33
York, Pa., 67
York County, 52, 68, 178; Codorus Township, 215
Yotter, Abraham. *See* Inventories

Zinzindorf, Count Nicholas von, 26
Zionsville, Pa., 189
Zoar, Ohio, 68